Woolly Worm Festival
Credit Todd Bush

Grandfather Mountain peaks
Credit Leslie Restivo
Grandfather Mountain

100

THINGS TO DO IN

NORTH CAROLINA

BEFORE YOU

DIE

100 THINGS TO DO IN NORTH CAROLINA BEFORE YOU DIE

KRISTY TOLLEY

Reedy Press
PO Box 5131
St. Louis, MO 63139, USA
reedypress.com

Library of Congress Control Number: 2025936733

ISBN: 9781681065946

Design by Jill Halpin

Cover photo courtesy of Leslie Restivo Grandfather Mountain

Unless otherwise noted, all photos are courtesy of the author or believed to be in the public domain.

Printed in the United States of America
25 26 27 28 29 5 4 3 2 1

CONTENTS

Music and Entertainment

Sports and Recreation

Culture and History

ACKNOWLEDGMENTS

I could not have written this book without the help and encouragement of family, friends, and colleagues.

A big thank-you goes to my husband, Joe, and my daughters, Peyton and Madden, who have accompanied me on countless adventures within North Carolina and beyond.

Many thanks to Scott Peacock and the staff at Visit NC for assisting me with photography, contacts, and countless other tasks to help ensure the accuracy of my content. Much gratitude is also extended to Craig Distl, who is such a fantastic advocate for the travel clients he represents. I have leaned on your expertise for many years, and I appreciate you so much. And to the North Carolina tourism partners and local business owners, thank you for your hospitality and for your help to make sure I paint an accurate picture of the unique and special places you represent.

Krispy Kreme
flagship store

PREFACE

In the middle of writing this book, Hurricane Helene, one of the deadliest US storms of the 21st century, caused unimaginable devastation across Western North Carolina. While many restaurants, hotels, and attractions have reopened, some areas are still recovering at the time of writing this preface in early 2025.

But if I've learned anything from all my travels within this remarkable state, it's that North Carolinians are a resilient and passionate bunch. The desire to share their beautiful state with others is strong, and it shows. Just notice the way a potter lights up when you ask how she became an artist or how excited your tour guide is to share local history.

And the wonderful thing about a North Carolina vacation is that it truly offers something for every type of traveler. Jonesing for a mountain getaway? Western North Carolina has you covered. Prefer the sun and sand? North Carolina's Atlantic coastline spans 320 miles. North Carolina brims with iconic attractions, "only here" experiences, and loads of fun things to do. From urban escapes to small-town visits, the Tar Heel State can satisfy all your travel cravings.

Forgive me if your favorite "must-see" didn't make this list. I did my best to offer up a variety of ways to experience this exceptional state, but narrowing the almost limitless allures of North Carolina to 100 was a nearly impossible task.

Whether you're touring North Carolina for the first time or the 50th time, I hope you let this book open the door to discovering places you didn't know about. In the back of the book, you'll find suggested itineraries, plus activities to consider based on the season of your visit.

Also, please share your North Carolina adventures with me on your social media via #100ThingsNC or tag me on your posts, and give me a follow on Instagram at @KristyTolley.

Mast General Store Candy

NC Apple Festival, Hendersonville
Credit Jared Kay

FOOD AND DRINK

1

FOLLOW THE TRAILS
TO GREAT EATS

I'm a firm believer that the best way to experience a destination is through its food, and North Carolina has something for every palate. A delicious way to sample the state's rich culinary offerings is through a food trail showcasing international favorites, local specialties, and beloved dishes passed down for generations. Grab a map and check off one or all.

A Southern heritage comfort food that dates back to the early 1800s, sonker is unique to North Carolina's Surry and Wilkes Counties and is the star of the Surry Sonker Trail. What's sonker? It's part fruit cobbler, part deep-dish pie—and all delicious.

Visit the farms and meet the cheese makers on the WNC Cheese Trail, which weaves through the mountains and foothills of Western North Carolina.

Jacksonville's International Food Trail, the Pitt County Brew & 'Cue Trail, and the NC Oyster Trail round out the list of "musts" for your epic foodie road trip.

Surry Sonker Trail
sonkertrail.org

WNC Cheese Trail
wnccheesetrail.org

NC Oyster Trail
ncoystertrail.org

International Food Trail
in Jacksonville
visitjacksonvillenc.com/189/
International-Food-Trail

Pitt County Brew & 'Cue Trail
visitgreenvillenc.com/restaurants/
pitt-county-brew-and-cue-trail

HERE ARE A FEW FOOD TOURS TO CONSIDER

If you'd prefer to have someone else lead you to North Carolina's best food spots, guided food tours led by locals are the way to go. Tour guides provide insight into the region's history, culture, and culinary scene, and the tours sometimes offer opportunities to meet the chefs and owners behind the dishes you taste.

Taste Carolina Gourmet Food Tours

919-237-2254
tastecarolina.net

Foodie Tours NC

910-713-1778
foodietoursnc.com

No Taste Like Home

828-209-8599
notastelikehome.org

2

FIND
YOUR FAVORITE BARBECUE

North Carolinians have strong opinions about their barbecue. Some stand by Eastern-style, which uses vinegar and pepper-based sauce on the meat (often after it's cooked). Others pledge allegiance to the Lexington-style barbecue, which features red sauce made with tomatoes, vinegar, and often, red pepper flakes.

The barbecue debate in North Carolina actually got political in 2006 when bills were introduced in both the House and Senate designating the Lexington Barbecue Festival the state's "official" barbecue festival. The Eastern-style camp countered that the declaration might unintentionally crown Lexington-style the state's barbecue king. The resulting compromise? The Lexington Barbecue Festival was designated the "Official Food Festival of the Piedmont Triad Region of the State of North Carolina."

Whichever way you lean, you just can't beat the unmistakable smoky flavor of pork that's slow roasted over wood or coals for hours. You can plate up your meat and two sides at a bevy of North Carolina barbecue joints, some serving folks for decades.

Whether you prefer Eastern-style or Lexington-style, there are loads of places to get your cue on across the state. Here are a few musts for your barbecue adventure.

Wilber's Barbecue

4172 US-70, Goldsboro, 919-778-5218
wilbersbbq.com

Hursey's Bar-B-Q

1834 S Church St., Burlington, 336-226-1694
hurseysbarbq.com

Red Bridges Barbecue Lodge

2000 E Dixon Blvd., Shelby, 704-482-8567
bridgesbbq.com

Lexington Barbecue

100 Smokehouse Ln., Lexington, 336-249-9814
lexbbq.com

The Barbecue Center

900 N Main St., Lexington, 336-248-4633
barbecuecenter.net

Stamey's Barbecue

2812 Battleground Ave., Greensboro, 336-288-9275
2206 W Gate City Blvd., Greensboro, 336-299-9888
stameys.com

Bum's Restaurant

566 E 3rd St., Ayden, 252-746-6880
bumsrestaurant.net

Clyde Cooper's Barbeque

327 S Wilmington St., Raleigh, 919-832-7614
clydecoopersbbq.com

Grady's BBQ

3096 Arrington Bridge Rd., Dudley, 919-735-7243
facebook.com/gradysbbqnc

3

RAISE A GLASS
AT NORTH CAROLINA WINERIES

While Napa Valley, California, might seem to get all the wine love in the US, North Carolina boasts an impressive winemaking history. The state is home to the country's oldest known living grapevine. Located on Roanoke Island, the "Mothervine" is estimated to be about 400 years old. It's believed the Mothervine was planted either by Croatan Native Americans or settlers of the Lost Colony.

North Carolina is home to about 250 wineries, offering everything from chardonnay and rosé to red blends and cabernet.

Established in 1975, Duplin Winery in Rose Hill is the state's oldest and largest winery. It specializes in wines made from the area's sweet scuppernong grapes.

For more muscadine and fruit wines, head to Locklear Vineyard & Winery in Maxton. Estate wines produced by the Native American–owned winery are made from fruit grown on the property. JOLO Winery & Vineyards is a lovely 80-acre property with a stunning view of Pilot Mountain. Their JOLO Pink rosé is one of my favorites (and often sells out quickly after it's released). NASCAR fans will want to check out Childress Vineyards, owned by former NASCAR driver Richard Childress. Western North Carolina is home to some excellent wineries with spectacular mountain views. They include Saint Paul Mountain Vineyards, Burntshirt Vineyards, Point Lookout Vineyards, and Biltmore Winery.

WINERY TOUR

It's easy to plan your route thanks to ncwine.org. The site provides a robust list of the state's wineries, as well as downloadable wine trail maps for every region.

Duplin Winery

505 N Sycamore St., Rose Hill, 910-289-3888
duplinwinery.com

Locklear Vineyard & Winery

1872 Preston Rd., Maxton, 910-316-0767
locklearwinery.com

JOLO Winery & Vineyards

219 JOLO Winery Ln., Pilot Mountain, 336-614-0030
jolovineyards.com

Childress Vineyards

1000 Childress Vineyards Rd., Lexington, 336-236-9463
childressvineyards.com

Saint Paul Mountain Vineyards

588 Chestnut Gap Rd., Hendersonville, 828-685-4002
saintpaulfarms.com

Burntshirt Vineyards

2695 Sugarloaf Rd., Hendersonville, 828-685-2402
burntshirtvineyards.com

Point Lookout Vineyards

408 Appleola Rd., Hendersonville, 828-808-8923
pointlookoutvineyards.com

Biltmore Winery

1 Lodge St., Asheville, 800-411-3812
biltmore.com/visit/winery

4

CHOW DOWN
ON CALABASH SEAFOOD

One of my most cherished childhood memories is our family's annual pilgrimage to Holden Beach for a week every summer. While wave jumping in the ocean and sandcastle building were primary pastimes, eating the best Calabash-style seafood each night brings me the most nostalgia. Our go-to spots were the Farmer's Daughter and Jane's Seafood (both long since closed).

Calabash-style seafood traces its beginnings to the 1930s in Calabash, North Carolina, often dubbed "The Seafood Capital of the World." Docks along the Calabash River teemed with fishing and shrimping boats. Local fishing families cooked up each day's fresh catch as soon as it came in. They dusted the seafood lightly with cornmeal instead of burying it in a heavy batter. This "Calabash style" method showcased the true flavors of the seafood.

The quaint family fish camps that lined the Calabash River evolved into restaurants. The first two, Coleman's Original and Beck's Restaurant, were opened in the 1940s by sisters Lucy Coleman and Ruth Beck. (Beck's is still owned and operated by the original family, but Coleman's closed in 2017 after a fire.)

Once you taste the light and flavorful goodness of Calabash-style seafood, you might not want it any other way.

MUST-VISITS FOR CALABASH-STYLE SEAFOOD

Many have been serving mouthwatering seafood dishes for decades.

Beck's Restaurant (since 1940)

1014 River Rd., Calabash, 910-579-6776
becksrestaurant.com

Holden Beach Seafood (since 1965)

2224 Holden Beach Rd. SW, Supply, 910-842-6276
holdenbeachseafood.com

The Boundary House

1045 River Rd., Calabash, 910-579-8888
boundaryhouserestaurant.com

Captain Nance's Seafood (since 1975)

9939 Nance St., Calabash, 910-579-2574
www.captainnancesseafood.com

Waterfront Seafood Shack

9945 Nance St., Calabash, 910-575-0017
waterfrontseafoodshack.com

5

TAKE A BITE
OUT OF THE NORTH CAROLINA APPLE FESTIVAL

Every Labor Day weekend since 1946, thousands of people make their way to historic downtown Hendersonville for one of North Carolina's biggest festivals. This festival showcases the area's thriving apple industry—Henderson County produces 85 percent of all apples grown in North Carolina. Here, the sweet aroma of cinnamon and apples permeates the air as visitors work their way along vendor booths teeming with homemade apple butter, cider, fresh-baked pies, and other goodies from local farms and orchards. Live music, entertainment, and rides add to the fun.

While you're in Hendersonville, raise a glass at one of the local cideries, such as Bold Rock Mills River, which sources local apples for their hard ciders, and Appalachian Ridge Artisan Hard Cider, situated in a 29-acre apple orchard.

318 N Main St., Ste. 15, Hendersonville, 828-697-4557
ncapplefestival.org

Bold Rock Mills River
72 School House Rd., Mills River, 828-595-9940
millsriver.boldrock.com

Appalachian Ridge Artisan Hard Cider
749 Chestnut Gap Rd., Hendersonville, 828-685-4002
saintpaulfarms.com/appalachian-ridge-hard-cider

TAKE A FOODIE ROAD TRIP

North Carolina is ripe with fantastic food festivals for every palate.

Highlands Food & Wine

highlandsfoodandwine.com

Lexington Barbecue Festival

1 N Main St., Lexington, 336-956-1880
thebarbecuefestival.com

The North Carolina Seafood Festival

412 D Evans St., Morehead City, 252-726-6273
ncseafoodfestival.org

North Carolina Peach Festival

214 S Main St., Candor, 910-974-4221
facebook.com/NCPeachFestival

Ayden Collard Festival

4144 West Ave., Ayden, 252-375-8095
aydencollardfestival.com

The North Carolina Strawberry Festival

Strawberry Event Field
Next to 809 N Brown St., Chadbourn
ncstrawberryfestival.com

Livermush Festival

58 Depot St., Marion, 828-652-2215
marionlivermushfestival.com

6

SAMPLE SWEET TRADITIONAL TREATS
AT MRS. HANES' MORAVIAN COOKIES

If you've never tasted the melt-in-your-mouth heavenly goodness that is a Moravian cookie, make haste to Winston-Salem. Better yet, get yourself to Mrs. Hanes' Moravian Cookies bakery to watch the sweet magic happen.

Moravian cookies, a beloved treat in Winston-Salem, trace their roots back to the 18th-century Moravian settlers from Central Europe. These settlers brought with them the tradition of baking ultra-thin, crisp cookies, often flavored with molasses, cinnamon, ginger, and cloves, resulting in a distinctive spicy-sweet taste.

Winston-Salem is home to several bakeries and shops that bake and sell Moravian cookies. However, Mrs. Hanes' is the only bakery that still fully rolls, cuts, and packs the cookies by hand. Bakery tours are offered Monday through Friday, where visitors get a behind-the-scenes look at the cookie-making process (and enjoy yummy samples throughout the tour).

Mrs. Hanes' has been family owned and operated for more than 100 years. The Hanes brood are a talented bunch, too. Beyond mouthwatering cookies, you can purchase beautiful pottery or carved hiking sticks handmade by family members.

4643 Friedberg Church Rd., Clemmons, 888-764-1402
hanescookies.com

FIND MORAVIAN COOKIES AND OTHER TRADITIONAL SPECIALTIES AT THESE LOCAL BAKERIES

Winkler Bakery

Winkler Bakery, located in the historic Old Salem district, is a must-visit. Established in 1807, it offers live demonstrations by bakers in traditional costume.

521 S Main St., Winston-Salem, 336-721-7302
oldsalem.org/winkler

Wilkerson Bakery

Wilkerson Bakery is a family-owned spot baking iconic Moravian cookies and other Moravian specialties since 1925.

593 S Stratford Rd., Winston-Salem, 336-829-0407
wilkersonbakery.com

Dewey's Bakery

You can stock up on Moravian cookies, cakes, and other bakery treats at a handful of Dewey's Bakery outposts. Dewey's has been a local staple since 1930.

Thruway Shopping Center
262 S Stratford Rd., Winston-Salem, 336-725-8321

Reynolda Manor
2876 Reynolda Rd., Winston-Salem, 336-724-0559

Friendly Shopping Center Greensboro
3326 W Friendly Ave., Ste. 128, Greensboro, 336-970-5711
deweys.com

LIFT YOUR SPIRITS
AT DISTILLERIES

North Carolina was the first Southern state to ban alcohol during Prohibition, which might have inspired bootleggers to pursue side hustles peddling their homemade concoctions.

Prohibition is long gone (cheers to that!), and we can savor our spirits in public at more than 80 distilleries in North Carolina. It would be impossible to list all the distilleries here, so I've chosen a handful of them across the state.

Piedmont Distillers, located in Madison, is North Carolina's first legal distillery since Prohibition. They are known for their Midnight Moon moonshine, created in collaboration with NASCAR legend Junior Johnson.

Call Family Distillers in Wilkesboro also celebrates its deep roots in moonshine history, with generations of craftsmanship distilled into their spirits. They specialize in traditional moonshine, paying homage to their storied past.

Muddy River Distillery in Mount Holly holds the title of North Carolina's first rum distillery. It's housed in the former Mount Holly Cotton Mill, the county's oldest existing mill still standing.

For an extensive list of North Carolina's distilleries, check out the Distillery Trail website at distillerytrail.com/directory-distillery/locations/north-carolina.

DISTILLERIES TO VISIT

Piedmont Distillers

3960 US-220, Madison, 336-445-0055
piedmontdistillers.com

Call Family Distillers

1611 Industrial Dr., Wilkesboro, 336-990-0708
callfamilydistillers.com

Muddy River Distillery

250 N Main St., Mount Holly, 704-820-8001
muddyriverdistillery.com

DID YOU KNOW?

We can thank moonshine for NASCAR. During Prohibition, bootleggers delivered their wares in souped-up cars designed to outrun federal agents. In the 1930s, moonshiners began to race their whiskey cars at local racetracks and fairgrounds. The races sometimes drew thousands of spectators willing to pay to see the show—and NASCAR was born. One of the most renowned moonshine runners-turned-race-car-drivers was Wilkes County native Junior Johnson, one of the first inductees into the NASCAR Hall of Fame.

GRAB A DOZEN
AT KRISPY KREME

While today it's an American icon, Krispy Kreme Doughnuts started small in North Carolina. Armed with a purchased yeast doughnut recipe from a New Orleans chef, Vernon Rudolph set up shop in a rented building on South Main Street in Winston-Salem (in what is now Historic Old Salem) in 1937.

Rudolph initially sold his baked goods to local grocery stores. However, passersby couldn't resist the alluring aroma of fresh-made pastries and began to stop and ask if they could buy the hot-from-the-oven glazed doughnuts. Vernon responded by cutting a hole in the building and selling the "hot and fresh" treats to customers on the sidewalk. People couldn't get enough, prompting Rudolph to open more locations in North Carolina and other Southeastern states.

Visit one of the original flagship shops on South Stratford Road to watch rows of hot, yeasty, sugary doughnuts roll through the glazing process. You just can't beat the taste of a just-made Krispy Kreme doughnut. And trust me, there's no way to prepare your taste buds for this experience.

259 S Stratford Rd., Winston-Salem, 336-724-2484
krispykreme.com

MORE PLACES FOR EPIC DOUGHNUTS

I'd be remiss if I didn't call out a few other must-visit spots across the state for an amazing doughnut. You'll definitely want to add these to your list!

Hole Doughnuts

168 Haywood Rd., Asheville, 828-774-5667
hole-doughnuts.com

Duck Donuts

1716 N Croatan Hwy., Kill Devil Hills, 252-480-3320
duckdonuts.com

Superior Bakery

2433 Hope Mills Rd., Fayetteville, 910-424-4242
superiorbakerync.com

Yummm Donut

2516 E Franklin Blvd., Ste. 9, Gastonia, 980-981-8989
facebook.com/YummmDonut

9

CAFFEINATE AND MAKE NEW FRIENDS

AT BITTY & BEAU'S COFFEE

Bitty & Beau's Coffee launched in Wilmington in 2016. It was the brainchild of Amy and Ben Wright, who wanted to create an inclusive business that employed mostly people with intellectual and developmental disabilities.

The coffee shop is the namesake of their two youngest children, who both have Down syndrome. The idea to open a coffee shop stemmed from a conversation the couple had about what the future held for Bitty and Beau as they grew into adulthood. Amy and Ben did a little research and discovered a jarring statistic: At the time, 80 percent of people with disabilities in the United States were unemployed.

Their solution? Create a "human rights movement disguised as a coffee shop" that would provide an environment that changes how people see others. Currently, Bitty & Beau's Coffee shops employ more than 400 people with disabilities.

The menu features a selection of hot and cold coffees and teas, plus frappés, smoothies, and baked goods.

They have a credit-card-only policy, which makes the transaction easier for the employees.

Bitty & Beau's employees make each visit special here—they are consistently kind, cheerful, and helpful.

For all things Bitty & Beau's, check out the Bitty & Beau's Coffee Show on YouTube, hosted by founders Amy and Ben Wright. Go to youtube.com/@thebittyandbeauscoffeeshow.

4949 New Centre Dr., Wilmington, 910-444-1944
1930 Camden Rd., Ste. 236, Charlotte, 980-299-2015
411 W 4th St., Winston-Salem, 336-553-7688
bittyandbeauscoffee.com

10

SIP CRAFT BEER
AT LOCAL BREWERIES

From the mountains to the coast, North Carolina's breweries are as diverse as its landscapes. Crisp lagers, hoppy IPAs, or experimental brews—there's something for every beer fan. Asheville earned the moniker "Beer City USA" thanks to over 55 breweries in its compact city limits, including iconic spots like Burial Beer Co. and Highland Brewing. Charlotte's brewery game is pretty strong, too. Olde Mecklenburg Brewery is known for its German-style lagers and a fantastic annual Christmas market. Sycamore Brewing offers a diverse range of crowd-pleasing brews and a lively outdoor space, and NoDa Brewing Company's creative seasonal brews are worth sampling. Travel east to the Outer Banks' Weeping Radish Brewery. It holds the distinction of being the state's first microbrewery, established in 1986.

Burial Beer Co.
40 Collier Ave., Asheville
828-475-2739
burialbeer.com

Highland Brewing
12 Old Charlotte Hwy., Asheville
828-299-3370
highlandbrewing.com

Olde Mecklenburg Brewery
4150 Yancey Rd., Charlotte
704-525-5644, ombbeer.com

Sycamore Brewing
2151 Hawkins St., Charlotte
980-201-3370
sycamorebrew.com

NoDa Brewing Company
150 W 32nd St., Charlotte
704-900-6851
nodabrewing.com

Weeping Radish
6810 Caratoke Hwy., Grandy
252-491-5205, weepingradish.com

NORTH CAROLINA BREWERY CRAWL

Lazy Hiker Brewing Company

188 W Main St., Franklin, 828-349-2337
lazyhikerbrewing.com

Broomtail Brewing

6404 Amsterdam Way, Wilmington, 910-209-4297
broomtailcraftbrewery.com

Fonta Flora Brewery

317 N Green St., Morganton, 828-475-7501
fontaflora.com

Neuse River Brewing & Brasserie

518 Pershing Rd., Raleigh, 984-232-8479
neuseriverbrewing.com

Forgotten Road Ales

141 E Harden St., Graham
forgottenroadales.com

11

SAVOR A FAMOUS FRIED PORK CHOP SANDWICH
AT SNAPPY LUNCH

Snappy Lunch is located in the charming hamlet of Mount Airy, the birthplace of Andy Griffith and the inspiration for the fictional town of Mayberry in *The Andy Griffith Show.*

It's more than just a popular dining spot—it's a slice of local history. Established in 1923, the restaurant has earned its place as a community staple, blending nostalgia with hearty Southern fare.

The restaurant's fame extends beyond Mount Airy, though. In an early episode of *The Andy Griffith Show*, Andy suggests to Barney that they grab a bite to eat at the Snappy Lunch, making it the only existing Mount Airy business to be mentioned in the show.

While there are loads of yummy dishes on the menu, the diner's World Famous Pork Chop Sandwich is its signature dish—a breaded pork chop sandwich topped with chili, coleslaw, onions, and mustard. It's a messy one, so make sure to ask for extra napkins.

125 N Main St., Mount Airy, 336-786-4931
thesnappylunch.com

12

RAISE THE ROOF

ON A BAR TOUR

Cap off a day of sightseeing in Asheville with a craft cocktail on a rooftop while taking in panoramic sunset views? Yes, please!

Add a couple more rooftops and pepper in a little local history, and you have a memorable and Instagram-worthy evening with friends. Each tour with Asheville Rooftop Bar Tours includes visits to some of the city's best rooftop restaurants and bars. Food is available at each stop, providing a great chance to sample each restaurant.

While you enjoy your cocktails and light bites, your guide opens a window to the past, sharing historical 19th-century and early 20th-century photos of bygone Asheville cityscapes. The Rooftop Sunset Tour and the Sky's the Limit Tour are available. If you don't drink alcohol (or are the designated driver for the evening), they have you covered! Each location also offers zero-proof mocktails.

45 S French Broad Ave., Ste. 170, Asheville, 828-774-7785
ashevillerooftopbartours.com

13

REFRESH YOURSELF
WITH A COLD CHEERWINE

Three cheers to L.D. Peeler! He created Cheerwine during World War I sugar shortages in 1917, when he used the uncommon wild cherry flavoring available from a traveling salesman to make his soda sweeter with less sugar. He chose the name Cheerwine to reflect the soft drink's effervescence and burgundy-red hue.

Cheerwine's slightly sweet black cherry flavor is distinct, and it pairs well with just about everything. New flavors have been introduced over the years, including Cheerwine Holiday Punch and Cheerwine Squeeze (a citrus-flavored soda).

You'll find Cheerwine in the soda sections of most grocery stores in the South, or you can make a pilgrimage to Salisbury, where it all began. Cheerwine factory tours aren't available, but you can snap a selfie at the original Cheerwine building at 300 East Council Street. Visit the headquarters location on Jake Alexander Boulevard and buy a drink or Cheerwine souvenir

Plan your visit to historic Salisbury around the Cheerwine Festival, held annually each spring. It features live music, food vendors, local artisans, and a copious supply of Cheerwine and Cheerwine-branded merchandise.

Cheerwine Headquarters (Carolina Beverage Corporation)
1413 Jake Alexander Blvd. S, Salisbury, 704-637-5881

Cheerwine Festival
cheerwinefest.com

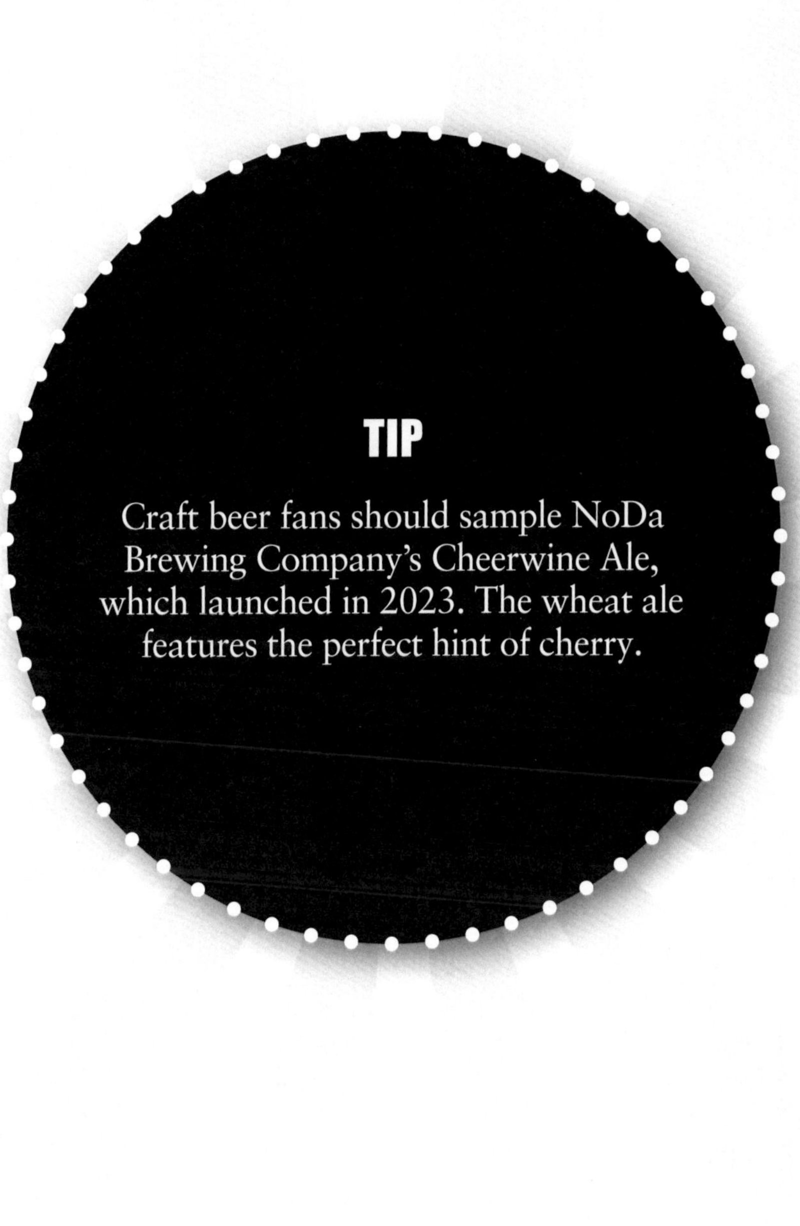

TIP

Craft beer fans should sample NoDa Brewing Company's Cheerwine Ale, which launched in 2023. The wheat ale features the perfect hint of cherry.

14

SHOP AND EAT LOCAL

AT A FARMERS MARKET

Perusing a local farmers market is a favorite weekend activity for many. Beyond your own hometown, it's also a fantastic way to connect with any town or city you visit. Here's a small sampling of markets in North Carolina worth checking out.

Raleigh's North Carolina State Farmers Public Market spans 30,000 square feet and is chock-full of plants, fresh produce, and homemade goods from local farms and artisans.

Charlotte Regional Farmers Market offers around 90 stalls manned by farmers and vendors who hail from the 15-county area surrounding Charlotte. Booths teem with local fruits, vegetables, hand-poured candles, and even prepared vegan food and fresh juices.

Established in 1977, Carrboro Farmers' Market is among the state's oldest local farmers markets, showcasing produce and artisan-made goods from around 75 local vendors.

The WNC Farmers Market features nearly 200 farmers and makers offering fresh produce, local honey, artwork, baked goods, and other items.

Stock up on pantry provisions at South Durham Farmers' Market. You'll also find a diverse selection of items such as hemp-based products, kimchi, and Southeast Asian vegetables.

NORTH CAROLINA FARMERS MARKETS

Don't forget to bring reusable bags for all your purchases. They're stronger than plastic bags and better for the environment!

North Carolina State Farmers Market

1201 Agriculture St., Raleigh, 919-733-7417
facebook.com/StateFarmersMarket

Charlotte Regional Farmers Market

1801 Yorkmont Rd., Charlotte, 704-357-1269
facebook.com/CharlotteRegionalFarmersMarket

Carrboro Farmers' Market

301 W Main St., Carrboro, 919-280-3326
carrborofarmersmarket.com

WNC Farmers Market

570 Brevard Rd., Asheville, 828-253-1691
facebook.com/wncfarmersmarket

South Durham Farmers' Market

500 Park Offices Dr., Durham, 984-377-7301
southdurhamfarmersmarket.com

15

COOL OFF WITH A CONE
AT TONY'S ICE CREAM COMPANY

Tony's Ice Cream Company is an essential stop for anyone visiting or traveling through Gastonia, just outside Charlotte. A local staple since 1915, it started as a modest dairy business delivering milk and ice cream to mill villages in the area. Over the years, the family-owned business evolved into a beloved local ice cream parlor, putting roots down on East Franklin Boulevard in 1947.

Choose from 28 flavors, including classics like vanilla, chocolate, and strawberry, plus specialties like banana pudding, black walnut, and almond joy. They also offer seasonal options that rotate throughout the year.

Beyond ice cream, Tony's serves hearty lunch items like burgers, hot dogs, and sandwiches, making it a perfect spot for a full meal or a quick snack.

604 E Franklin Blvd., Gastonia, 704-867-7085
tonysicecream.com

OTHER NORTH CAROLINA ICE CREAM SHOPS

Yum Yum Better Ice Cream and Hot Dogs

1219 Spring Garden St., Greensboro, 336-272-8284
facebook.com/yumyumbettericecreamandhotdogs

Pike's Old Fashioned Soda Shop

1930 Camden Rd., Charlotte, 704-372-0092
pikessodashop.net

Dolly's Dairy Bar (open seasonally)

128 Pisgah Hwy., Pisgah Forest, 828-862-6610

The Parlour

117 Market St., Durham, 919-564-7999
theparlour.co

Calabash Creamery

9910 Beach Dr. SW, Calabash, 910- 575-1180
calabashcreamery.com

Howling Cow Dairy Education Center and Creamery

100 Dairy Ln., Raleigh, 919-513-4695
howlingcow.ncsu.edu

Horseback Jousting at the Carolina Renaissance Festival
Credit Carolina Renaissance Festival

MUSIC AND ENTERTAINMENT

TAP YOUR TOES
AT MERLEFEST

It began as a fundraiser for a local community college in 1988. Today, it's one of the country's premier music festivals. The first MerleFest was organized to raise money for Wilkes Community College's horticulture department to create the campus's Garden of the Senses. The school's lead horticulturist asked local resident and bluegrass legend Doc Watson to perform. He agreed to, under the condition that the garden pay homage to his son, Merle, who died in a tractor accident in 1985 at the age of 36.

More than 75,000 festival-goers converge on Wilkesboro the last weekend of April each year. The festival celebrates "traditional plus" music—a blend of bluegrass, country, folk, blues, and more—featuring performances by a mix of renowned artists and emerging talents across multiple stages.

MerleFest has hosted legendary acts like Alison Krauss, the Avett Brothers, and Dolly Parton alongside a diverse array of musicians who embody the spirit of Appalachian music. The festival also offers workshops, family-friendly activities, food vendors, and an artisan craft market.

1328 S Collegiate Dr., Wilkesboro, 800-343-7857
merlefest.org

OTHER NORTH CAROLINA MUSIC FESTIVALS

Carolina Beach Music Festival

Cape Fear Blvd. and Carolina Beach Ave. S, Carolina Beach
910-458-8434
facebook.com/CarolinaBeachMusicFestival

North Carolina Folk Festival

200 N Davie St., Ste. 401, Greensboro
336-265-6943
ncfolkfestival.com

Hopscotch Music Festival

Downtown Raleigh
hopscotchmusicfest.com

Ol' Front Porch Music Festival

605 South Ave., Oriental
252-220-2281
olfrontporch.org

17

CATCH A SHOW
AT A HISTORIC THEATER

Constructed in 1858, Thalian Hall in Wilmington is one of the oldest community theaters in America. The building once housed the library, the town government, and an opera house, giving it the unique distinction of serving as both Wilmington's political and cultural center.

Renamed Thalian Hall Center for the Performing Arts in 1986, Thalian Hall is a remarkable example of 19th-century architecture, with intricate plasterwork and elegant columns. The main auditorium exudes historic charm with lush red velvet seats, rich green walls, and a spectacular chandelier.

Thalian Hall hosted a slew of major artists in the 19th and early 20th centuries, such as Lillian Russell and Buffalo Bill Cody. Today, the theater remains a cornerstone for the performing arts in Wilmington, serving as a venue for local and national performers, with a wide range of theatrical productions, concerts, and other cultural events.

310 Chestnut St., Wilmington, 910-632-2285, thalianhall.org

TIP

In the lobby of the theater, you'll find a piece of Thalian Hall's legacy on display—the original drop curtain that hung onstage when the theater opened in 1858.

FIND FUN AND THRILLS
AT CAROWINDS

We lived within about a five-minute drive to Carowinds for many years. When our daughters were younger, we made the most out of our season pass every single summer, spending countless days in the theme park or cooling off at the water park.

The 407-acre theme park features several areas, such as the Thrill Zone with heart-pumping roller coasters like Fury 325, North America's tallest and fastest giga coaster. Families will love Camp Snoopy, inspired by the beloved Peanuts characters, offering kid-friendly rides and attractions. Also, Blue Ridge Junction oozes with Appalachian-themed charm (check out Copperhead Strike, the first double-launch coaster in the Carolinas). The Carolina Harbor Waterpark has wave pools, lazy rivers, and exhilarating waterslides.

14523 Carowinds Blvd., Charlotte, 704-588-2600
carowinds.com

TIP

Carowinds straddles the North Carolina–South Carolina border, so you can actually stand in two states at once.

FOLLOW THE YELLOW BRICK ROAD

AT LAND OF OZ THEME PARK

Tucked in the North Carolina mountains, this destination is certainly no place like home. The Land of Oz theme park opened in Beech Mountain 1970 to pay homage to L. Frank Baum's book The Wonderful World of Oz and the timeless 1939 movie it inspired, *The Wizard of Oz*.

The park boasted the Emerald City amphitheater stage, a roller coaster, gift shops, a balloon ride, a reproduction of Dorothy's family farmhouse, and the iconic Yellow Brick Road. The Land of Oz was a popular family attraction until it closed in 1980. Many of the original structures were demolished in the mid to late '80s after repeated vandalism and disrepair.

However, beginning in 1988, original park employees known as "Ozzies" launched efforts to reopen the park each year for what eventually became known as the Autumn at Oz Festival. The immersive festival typically takes place over three weekends in September, and features food and craft vendors, a petting zoo, special exhibits, and live performances. Visitors can skip along the Yellow Brick Road with Dorothy, the Scarecrow, the Cowardly Lion, and the Tin Man.

1 Yellow Brick Rd., Beech Mountain, 844-307-7469
landofoznc.com

20

EAT AND PLAY
AT THE NORTH CAROLINA STATE FAIR

Every October in Raleigh, you can get your fried-food-on-a-stick fix and so much more at the North Carolina State Fair. More than one million visitors descend on the state fairgrounds each year. The fair showcases North Carolina's agricultural heritage with 4-H booths, plus exhibits featuring innovations in farming and technology.

There's also no shortage of carnival games, rides, and a bustling midway. The wafting smell of fair food is hard to resist, so just give in. As you meander the fairgrounds, nosh on traditional favorites like funnel cakes, corn dogs, cotton candy, and roasted peanuts. Stop and cheer on folks vying for the top prize in pie baking or the biggest pumpkin competition.

4285 Trinity Rd., Raleigh, 919-821-7400
ncagr.gov/divisions/ncstatefair

BROADEN YOUR MUSICAL HORIZONS AT THE NORTH CAROLINA MUSIC HALL OF FAME

For a dive into North Carolina's rich musical heritage, pay a visit to the North Carolina Music Hall of Fame in Kannapolis. The museum showcases the talented artists who have significant ties to the Tar Heel State, as well as those who have richly contributed to the world of music. Peruse a robust variety of exhibits that honor musicians from different genres, including country, gospel, rock, jazz, and hip-hop. You'll find ephemera, photographs, and instruments belonging to inducted artists. Notable items on display include Randy Travis's cowboy hat, Roberta Flack's piano, and James Taylor's guitar. In addition to its permanent exhibits, the North Carolina Music Hall of Fame hosts special events and live performances throughout the year, plus educational programs and workshops for music enthusiasts of all ages.

600 Dale Earnhardt Blvd., Kannapolis, 704-934-2320
northcarolinamusichalloffame.org

TIP

The museum is open Monday through Friday. Admission is free, but donations are encouraged.

SHOUT "HUZZAH!"
AT THE RENAISSANCE FESTIVAL

Gather your lords and ladies and toast to your good health with a pint and a turkey leg at the North Carolina Renaissance Festival. This lively festival takes place in Huntersville Saturdays and Sundays in October and November each year, and it's one of my favorite autumn events.

It's easy to lose yourself in medieval times here thanks to over 20 acres of immersive entertainment, including jousting tournaments, royal feasts, and live stage performances. Roam the grounds for handcrafted goods or just enjoy bantering with costumed characters walking the festival grounds. (You might even meet Queen Isabella!)

Don't be surprised if you see festivalgoers going all in with 16th-century-style costumes. And if you feel left out, no worries! Several artisans are on hand selling everything from gypsy dresses and kilts to fairy hair garlands and leather bags.

16445 Poplar Tent Rd., Huntersville, 704-896-5555
carolina.renfestinfo.com

23

WATCH A HISTORY MYSTERY

AT THE LOST COLONY

First performed in 1937, The Lost Colony is America's longest-running outdoor symphonic drama. Written by Pulitzer Prize–winning playwright Paul Green, this captivating play reenacts the mystery of the Roanoke Colony, England's first attempt at permanent settlement in the New World.

Set in 1587, the story follows 117 settlers who vanished without a trace, leaving behind only the enigmatic word "CROATOAN" carved into a post. This unsolved historical puzzle is brought to life with a blend of drama, music, and choreography, captivating audiences under the open sky of Waterside Theatre in Manteo on the Outer Banks.

The play runs most evenings from late spring through the summer. The outdoor theater's location offers panoramic views of Roanoke Sound, enhancing the dramatic ambiance.

1409 National Park Dr., Manteo, 252-473-6000
thelostcolony.org

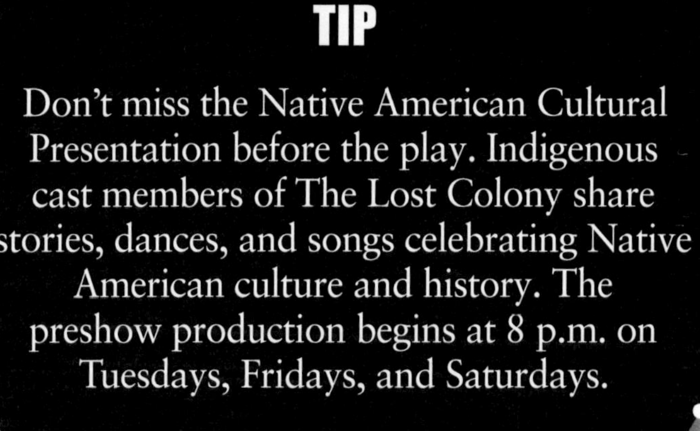

TIP

Don't miss the Native American Cultural Presentation before the play. Indigenous cast members of The Lost Colony share stories, dances, and songs celebrating Native American culture and history. The preshow production begins at 8 p.m. on Tuesdays, Fridays, and Saturdays.

24

HAVE THE TIME OF YOUR LIFE
IN LAKE LURE

Sequestered by the Blue Ridge Mountains, Lake Lure's pristine waters and picturesque landscapes have drawn travelers for decades. But movie buffs might be attracted to Lake Lure for another reason: Parts of the 1987 movie *Dirty Dancing* were filmed there.

Splash around Lake Lure Beach and Water Park, where Johnny and Baby's iconic "lake lift" scene was filmed (extra points if you re-create the movie scene while you're there). Chill out on the beach, hit the park's waterslide, or join a guided boat tour.

Book a stay at the Lake Lure Inn & Spa. Built in 1927, the historic hotel housed Patrick Swayze, Jennifer Grey, and other cast and crew members during filming. (Other notable guests include F. Scott Fitzgerald and Franklin D. Roosevelt.)

Lake Lure has even hosted an annual Dirty Dancing Festival every fall since 2010. However, in 2023, the town was forced to rename it the Lake Lure Dance Festival, due to contractual obligations required by the studio that owns the rights to the movie. Whatever the festival is called, it's chock-full of dancing, live music, watermelon games, and even a lake lift competition.

Lake Lure Inn & Spa
2771 Memorial Hwy., Lake Lure, 828-625-2525
lakelurenc.com

TIP

Stretch your legs at Chimney Rock Park, just a short three-mile drive from Lake Lure. Hike to the top of the towering 315-foot monolith for jaw-dropping views of the Hickory Nut Gorge and Lake Lure. The park also features several other trails, including one that leads to the beautiful Hickory Nut Falls. The 404-foot waterfall was featured in another memorable movie, The Last of the Mohicans.

chimneyrockpark.com

25

TALK TO THE ANIMALS
AT THE NORTH CAROLINA ZOO

Opened in 1974 and spanning over 2,600 acres, Asheboro's North Carolina Zoo and Botanical Gardens is the world's largest natural habitat zoo. Here, more than 1,700 animals roam in spacious, naturalistic environments, mimicking their native habitats.

Visitors can explore exhibits themed around two continents: Africa and North America. The African region features majestic creatures like lions, elephants, and gorillas. It's also where you'll find the Giraffe Deck, an elevated platform that allows you to get eye-to-eye with the graceful giants. The North American region showcases grizzly bears, cougars, and native birds. The desert habitat houses meerkats, sand cats, and a variety of reptiles, including lizards and snakes.

If one day there isn't enough time, stay overnight. The zoo offers Snorin' Safaris camping adventures in the spring, which includes an evening stroll through the zoo, s'mores by a campfire, and other activities.

4401 Zoo Pkwy., Asheboro, 800-488-0444, nczoo.org

TIP

A new 10-acre Asia Continent is currently under construction and scheduled to open in 2026. The area will highlight species such as tigers, Komodo dragons, white- cheeked gibbons, and other animals.

26

DELVE INTO BLUEGRASS MUSIC
AT EARL SCRUGGS CENTER

Situated in the heart of Shelby, Earl Scruggs Center is housed in the restored 1907 Cleveland County Courthouse. The museum celebrates the life and legacy of Earl Scruggs, a legendary banjo player who revolutionized bluegrass music with his three-finger picking style. Born in 1924 in Cleveland County, Scruggs gained fame as part of the bluegrass duo Flatt and Scruggs and contributed significantly to the genre, helping popularize bluegrass music across the country and throughout the world.

Interactive exhibits here explore Scruggs's influence on American music, the history of bluegrass, and the cultural heritage of the region. Visitors can engage with music demonstrations, artifacts, and multimedia displays that bring the story of bluegrass to life.

The center also hosts various events, including live performances, educational workshops, and community gatherings, making it a vibrant hub for music enthusiasts and a testament to Earl Scruggs's enduring impact on the music industry.

103 S Lafayette St., Shelby, 704-487-6233
earlscruggscenter.org

27

CELEBRATE THE HOLIDAYS

AT THE OMNI GROVE PARK INN NATIONAL GINGERBREAD HOUSE COMPETITION

It started as a modest display of gingerbread houses created by local residents in 1992. Today, this Asheville tradition is the world's largest gingerbread competition.

Gingerbread crafters across the country pour their hearts, souls, and loads of sugar into their creations in hopes of snagging a portion of the $40,000 in cash and prizes. While it's not mandatory that entries be a house-style structure, they must be entirely edible and 75 percent gingerbread.

The competition takes place each November. If you miss the competition, no worries! The aromatic and beautiful display of gingerbread entries typically remains at the resort from mid-November to early January. Those not staying at the resort can visit on select dates, anytime Monday through Thursday or after 6 p.m. on Sunday.

290 Macon Ave., Asheville, 800-438-5800
omnihotels.com/hotels/asheville-grove-park

28

LIGHT UP THE HOLIDAYS
IN MCADENVILLE

Fittingly dubbed "Christmas Town U.S.A.," McAdenville is transformed into a glittering Christmas wonderland each winter. The enchanting tradition began in 1956 when the local community decided to spread holiday cheer by decorating nine trees around the McAdenville Community Center. Over the decades, the event has grown exponentially in scale and popularity.

More than 600,000 people make their way to McAdenville each holiday to ooh and ah over the more than 500,000 lights illuminating around 160 houses and numerous public buildings along with the town's lake and several churches.

The light displays typically run the entire month of December. Visitors can stroll through the streets or drive along the route.

100 Main St., McAdenville, 704-823-2333
facebook.com/ChristmasTownUSA

Beech Mountain

SPORTS AND RECREATION

EXPLORE
THE GREAT SMOKY MOUNTAINS BY RAIL

Operating since the late 1890s, the Great Smoky Mountains Railroad lets you soak in striking landscapes as you travel through the Nantahala National Forest, the Great Smoky Mountains National Park, and along Fontana Lake.

Trips run year-round, showcasing nature's beauty in every season. Specialty excursions offered throughout the year include the Uncorked Wine Train and the Smoky Mountain Beer Run. Family trips like the Bunny Hopper Express (on Easter weekend) and the Polar Express train ride (runs November and December) are wildly popular, and tickets sell out quickly.

45 Mitchell St., Bryson City, 800-872-4681
gsmr.com

TIP

Extend your time in Bryson City with an overnight stay at a historic hotel. Calhoun House Inn & Suites and Fryemont Inn were both constructed in the early 1920s and provide a charming retreat for your time in the mountains.

HANG OUT
AT HANGING ROCK

Outdoor enthusiasts and nature lovers will appreciate Sauratown Mountains' dramatic cliffs and rock formations. Perhaps its most recognizable is Hanging Rock. It's situated within Hanging Rock State Park, which is 25 miles east of Pilot Mountain and connected to Pilot Mountain State Park by the Sauratown Trail.

Over 20 miles of trails await hikers, and many lead to various waterfalls, caves, and scenic overlooks. Among them is the Hanging Rock Trail, a moderate 2.6-mile (round trip) hike that rewards hikers with panoramic vistas at the summit.

Rock climbing, fishing, swimming, and camping are other ways to pass your time in Hanging Rock State Park. It's also a haven for bird-watchers and wildlife photographers, with abundant flora and fauna.

1790 Hanging Rock Park Rd., Danbury, 336-593-8480
ncparks.gov/state-parks/hanging-rock-state-park

DID YOU KNOW?

Hanging Rock State Park holds historical significance. It was developed in the 1930s by the Civilian Conservation Corps as one of the New Deal programs, which built many of the park's original facilities. The park's bathhouse was added to the National Register of Historic Places in 1991.

31

RIDE THE RAPIDS AND MORE

AT THE U.S. NATIONAL WHITEWATER CENTER

Although its Olympic-caliber training facilities are used by athletes preparing for international competitions, you don't have to be an Olympic athlete to love the U.S. National Whitewater Center.

Located in Charlotte, the 1,300-acre center is home to the world's largest man-made whitewater river. Whitewater rafting isn't the only fun to be had here. The center offers tons of activities, such as kayaking, paddleboarding, rock climbing, mountain biking, and hiking. In the winter you can ice-skate, play hockey, or try your hand at cask curling, a fun twist on traditional curling as you slide mini kegs across the ice and compete for points.

Annual events like Tuck Fest and Flow Fest are extremely well attended. Tuck Fest is a multiday festival with competitions, live music, and workshops. Flow Fest focuses on wellness, offering yoga, mindfulness activities, and holistic workshops in a pristine outdoor setting.

5000 Whitewater Center Pkwy., Charlotte, 704-391-3900
whitewater.org

TIP

Another Whitewater Center, Whitewater Pisgah, is located within the Pisgah National Forest in Western North Carolina. It offers mountain biking, fishing, climbing, trail running, plus whitewater and flatwater paddling within the more than 500,000 acres of public land.

5289 N Mills River Rd., Mills River, 704-391-3900
pisgah.whitewater.org

32

GET SPOOKED
ON A GHOST TOUR

I'm a sucker for a good spine-chilling yarn. Drop me into a city at dusk with a costumed tour guide and I'm in heaven. Ghost tours offer a fantastic and fun way to learn about the city you're visiting. North Carolina sure has its share of stories to tell—from scandals and unsolved murders to haunted theaters and mysterious events. A number of tour companies across the state offer spooky insight into local lore.

Raleigh Ghosts takes you through the heart of downtown Raleigh, where you'll hear about haunted theaters, eerie hotels, and unexplained happenings in the state's capital.

Haunted Wilmington delves into the coastal city's ghostly past, with visits to sites like the 1770 Burgwin-Wright House, built on the ballast stone walls of the former city jail.

Pirates, ghost ships, and Civil War spirits come to life during a Beaufort Ghost Walk tour of North Carolina's third-oldest town. You'll also visit the historic Old Burying Ground, where you just might hear the rum keg girl humming near her grave.

TIP

Not sure you want to commit to a tour but still interested in haunted history? If you find yourself in an old local bar, historic hotel, or even a restaurant housed in a renovated factory building, ask the staff if it's haunted. They just might have a few terrifying tales to share.

GHOST TOURS TO TRY

Raleigh Ghosts

1 E Edenton St., Raleigh
usghostadventures.com/raleigh-ghost-tour

Haunted Wilmington

8 Market St., Wilmington, 910-794-1866
hauntedwilmington.com

Beaufort Ghost Walk

108 Middle Ln., Beaufort, 252-772-9925
pctourco.com/beaufort-ghost-walk

CATCH
THE SHADOW OF THE BEAR

Every autumn, throngs of visitors gather along Highway 64 in the Blue Ridge Mountains to witness the Shadow of the Bear. The phenomenon occurs when sunlight hits the mountain at just the right angle, casting a perfect silhouette of a giant black bear across the colorful landscape.

From mid-October through early November, the shadow appears for about 30 minutes each day between 5:30 and 6:15 p.m. The Rhodes Big View Overlook on Highway 64 provides a good vantage point from which to view the event.

While the shadow is an ephemeral phenomenon, it's worth planning a visit if you're in the area. Whether you're hiking or just stopping for the view, the Shadow of the Bear is a great reminder of how nature can create surprising and beautiful moments.

TIP

You can also view the Shadow of the Bear from mid-February to early March, so you'll have fewer crowds to contend with. The trade-off? The trees won't be ablaze in vibrant fall colors, which certainly adds to the experience.

GLAMP LIKE A CHAMP IN THE MOUNTAINS

Glamping is the sweet spot for those who like the idea of camping, but you require more comfort than a forest floor provides. North Carolina's upscale and unique camping spots run the gamut, from contemporary cabins to vintage Airstreams.

Asheville River Cabins offers a rustic yet chic experience within a lush natural forest just minutes from Asheville's bustling downtown. Accommodations come with a host of amenities, such as a full kitchen, smart TVs, and cozy fire pits.

In nearby Clyde, the 160-acre mountaintop refuge that is The Glamping Collective provides a unique selection of accommodations. Each site is thoughtfully designed with upscale touches such as king-size beds and private hot tubs.

JuneBug Retro Resort in Weaverville provides a nostalgic twist with its collection of restored vintage trailers, complete with modern comforts like AC, microwaves, and coffee makers.

Asheville River Cabins
318 Wanderlust Ridge, Arden, 828-684-9147
ashevillerivercabins.com

The Glamping Collective
2504 Crabtree Mountain Rd., Clyde, 828-492-3620
theglampingcollective.com

JuneBug Retro Resort
355 Clarks Chapel Rd., Weaverville, 828-208-1979
junebugretroresort.com

35

PEDAL YOUR WAY
ON THE RAIL IN ANDREWS VALLEY

If you're looking for an out-of-the-box way to explore North Carolina's gorgeous Appalachian countryside, hit the rails! Andrews Valley Rail Tours is the state's first rail-bike tour company, offering 8.5-mile round-trip guided rail cart tours using motorized vehicles that travel along the historic Murphy Branch rail line.

Tours begin at the Historic Andrews Train Depot, a beautifully restored 1907 building that once served as a hub for local commerce and travel. The depot now houses a museum and a gift shop stocked with drinks, snacks, sunscreen, T-shirts, hats, magnets, and various sundries. If you forgot to bring one, coolers are also available to rent or buy.

You'll ride the rail amid scenic landscapes, including picturesque farmland, lush forests, the tranquil Valley River, and a stone tunnel hand-carved by workers from Southern Railway in 1894.

345 Locust St., Andrews, 828-557-4021
andrewsvalleyrailtours.com

GRAB A KILT AND HEAD
TO THE HIGHLAND GAMES

Each July, the Grandfather Mountain Highland Games celebrates Scottish heritage and honors the legacy of the Scottish immigrants who settled in North Carolina and other parts of the Appalachian region. Since its debut in 1956, the festival has become one of the country's largest Scottish festivals.

The Highland Games feature an exciting array of traditional Scottish athletic events like the caber toss, hammer throw, weight toss for height, and the sheaf toss, where athletes demonstrate incredible strength and skill. There are also piping and drumming competitions, along with Highland dancing and the opportunity to watch clan gatherings and historical reenactments.

In addition to the athletic feats, visitors can enjoy Scottish food, drink, and craft vendors, making the Highland Games a must for anyone interested in Scottish culture and mountain heritage. Whether you're a competitor or a spectator, it's an event that brings the spirit of Scotland to the heart of North Carolina.

MacRae Meadows, Blowing Rock Hwy., Linville, 828-733-1333
gmhg.org

37

HIT THE SLOPES
AT AREA SKI RESORTS

North Carolina boasts several fantastic ski areas, offering diverse slopes for all skill levels amid stunning mountain views.

Appalachian Ski Mountain has been operating since 1962. This family-owned-and-run ski resort is ideal for beginners and families with younger kids. With 13 runs, it's smaller than other area resorts and extremely easy to navigate.

Because it's the highest ski area in the eastern US, Beech Mountain Resort boasts a more natural snowfall and chillier temperatures—ideal elements for optimum skiing conditions. And with 95 skiable acres, there's plenty of room to spread out. The resort is reminiscent of a charming Bavarian village—which makes for a prime Instagram backdrop.

With 20 trails, 125 skiable acres, and a popular terrain park, Sugar Mountain Resort in Banner Elk claims the title as the largest ski resort in North Carolina. It's also home to the only double black diamond slope and the largest vertical drop (1,200 feet) in the state.

Not a skier or snowboarder? Ice-skating, snowshoeing, and tubing are plentiful at the above ski resorts.

Smaller ski resorts can provide a more intimate and less crowded experience for beginner skiers. Cataloochee Ski Area, Hatley Pointe, and Sapphire Valley Resort are ideal for families, as well as for beginner and intermediate skiers.

NORTH CAROLINA SKI RESORTS

Appalachian Ski Mountain

940 Ski Mountain Rd., Blowing Rock
828-295-7828
appskimtn.com

Beech Mountain Resort

1007 Beech Mountain Pkwy., Beech Mountain
800-438-2093
beechmountainresort.com

Sugar Mountain Resort

1009 Sugar Mountain Dr., Sugar Mountain
800-784-2768
skisugar.com

Cataloochee Ski Area

1080 Ski Lodge Rd., Maggie Valley
828-926-0285
cataloochee.com

Hatley Pointe

578 Valley View Cir., Mars Hill
828-689-4111
hatleypointe.com

Sapphire Valley Resort

127 Cherokee Trl., Sapphire
828-743-7663
skisapphirevalley.com

GET CAUGHT UP
IN A CLASSIC ACC BASKETBALL RIVALRY

ACC basketball ignites passion like few other rivalries, and at the heart of it all is the Carolina–Duke clash.

The Dean E. Smith Center, affectionately known as the "Dean Dome," is a sea of Carolina blue. More than 20,000 fans create a deafening roar, their energy fueling the University of North Carolina at Chapel Hill (UNC) Tar Heels. The arena's history echoes with legendary moments, each game adding a new chapter to the rivalry.

Then there's Cameron Indoor Stadium, a cauldron of intensity. Duke University's home is a smaller, more intimate venue, where the student section known as the "Cameron Crazies" are a force of nature. Their chants and unwavering support create an intimidating atmosphere for any opponent, especially the Tar Heels.

Whether it's the expansive Dean Dome or the charged atmosphere of Cameron, a Carolina–Duke game is an unforgettable experience. The stakes are always high, the competition fierce, and the memories last a lifetime.

TIP

Carve out time for a visit to the Carolina Basketball Museum, located on the University of North Carolina campus in Chapel Hill. It features an impressive selection of memorabilia, historical artifacts, championship trophies, and interactive displays that highlight the team's legacy and iconic players like Michael Jordan. You don't have to be a basketball fan to appreciate the rich history and achievements of the Tar Heels basketball program.

39

BE A BEACH BUM

With around 320 miles of ocean shoreline, North Carolina is blessed with gorgeous stretches of sand on which to relax and play. From laid-back spots to chill to areas rich in outdoor activities, each coastal region has its own distinct charm and vibe to match your vacation style.

Topsail Island is a serene getaway known for its long stretches of sandy beaches and tranquil waters. It's ideal for families and those seeking a peaceful retreat, with plenty of opportunities for shelling and spotting sea turtles.

Outer Banks' 200-mile-long string of barrier islands is known for its windswept dunes, historic lighthouses, and wild horses. Active travelers can kiteboard, surf, or explore the landscape via horseback.

In the Northern Outer Banks, Currituck is known for its peaceful beaches and historical sites, including the Currituck Beach Lighthouse. It offers a laid-back vibe, perfect for couples and families looking for a quiet escape.

Wilmington blends historic charm with vibrant beach life. At nearby Wrightsville, Carolina, and Kure beaches, vacationers have access to both city attractions and beachside relaxation.

The Brunswick Islands feature family-friendly beaches like Sunset Beach and Holden Beach, where you can slow down and kick back. Plenty of fishing piers and golf courses offer other seaside diversions. You can also get your fill of Calabash-style seafood.

Divers should head to the Crystal Coast. Its clear waters offer unique year-round diving opportunities. Water temperatures range from 75 to 80 degrees in the summer and fall, making it an ideal spot for warmwater wreck diving. The Emerald Isle, Atlantic Beach areas, and Pine Knoll Shores are also worth a visit.

Topsail Island
topsailchamber.org

Outer Banks
outerbanks.org

Northern Outer Banks
visitcurrituck.com

Brunswick Islands
ncbrunswick.com

Crystal Coast
crystalcoastnc.org

Emerald Isle
emeraldisle-nc.org

Atlantic Beach
atlanticbeach-nc.com

40

STAY IN A GEM

For more than 80 years, savvy travelers have relied on the AAA Diamond rating. Top-notch amenities, upscale rooms, and unparalleled hospitality are all hallmarks of hotels earning an elusive AAA Five Diamond rating. The Umstead Hotel and Spa in Cary is currently North Carolina's only AAA Five Diamond hotel. This oasis earned its prestigious AAA Five Diamond rating within a year of its opening in 2007 and has maintained it ever since. Situated on 18 acres of wooded landscape, The Umstead is convenient to area attractions yet tucked away to offer privacy for an intimate getaway. Choose from among 150 rooms and suites dressed in serene hues, privately curated artwork, and moss-soft carpeting. The spa-style marble bathrooms feature a deep soaking tub and separate shower. Grab an art tour brochure from the concierge and explore the hotel's extensive collection.

100 Woodland Pond Dr., Cary, 919-447-4000
theumstead.com

TIP

Make sure to reserve a table at The Umstead's signature restaurant, Herons, the only AAA Five Diamond and Forbes Five Star restaurant in North Carolina. Chef Steven Greene, a James Beard "Best Chef: Southeast" semifinalist, is at the helm. Savor distinctive dishes, such as elk loin with chestnut polenta, squash, confit quince, and baby turnips; and dry-aged duck with farro verde, sweet potato, blood orange, coconut, and hoisin jus.

JOURNEY TO THE HIGHEST POINT IN NORTH CAROLINA

At 6,684 feet above sea level, Mount Mitchell is North Carolina's highest point and the highest peak east of the Mississippi River. The mountain is named for Elisha Mitchell, the first person to calculate the summit's height using barometric readings and math in 1835. His grave site is at the summit. Immerse yourself in fragrant canopies of spruce and fir, and abundant wildflowers like the purple-fringed orchid, ox-eye daisy, and pink turtlehead. Mount Mitchell is also home to diverse wildlife, including bobcats, whitetail deer, and around 91 species of birds. Several trails lead to the mountaintop, and there's a path for every skill level—from easy to strenuous. The summit rewards climbers with remarkable 360-degree views that span some 85 miles. A shop, a museum, and restroom facilities are located at the summit. A restaurant is open seasonally, from spring to fall.

2388 NC 128, Burnsville, 828-867-4000
ncparks.gov/state-parks/mount-mitchell-state-park

TIP

Not a hiker? You can reach almost all the way to the summit by car. Near the top you'll find a parking area. From there, head to the observation deck along a short paved trail.

EXPLORE
GRANDFATHER MOUNTAIN

When Hugh Morton inherited Grandfather Mountain from his own grandfather in in 1952, he knew the more than 4,500-acre portion of land was something to be treasured and shared. He quickly extended the existing single-lane road into a two-lane road and brainstormed the Mile High Swinging Bridge. Later, to ensure the preservation of Grandfather Mountain, he gifted conservation easements of over 3,000 acres to the Nature Conservancy. Grandfather Mountain was recognized as a member of the international network of Biosphere Reserves by UNESCO in 1992.

This iconic North Carolina landmark earned its name from its distinct profile, which resembles a grandfather's face in repose.

Grandfather Mountain has 11 trails for hikers of all levels, ranging from gentle strolls to challenging climbs. The two-mile Raven Rocks Loop winds through forests and past rock formations; while the challenging 4.3-mile Grandfather Trail to Calloway Peak rewards hikers with spectacular views of the surrounding mountains.

Yonni's Clubhouse, which opened in 2025, is an immersive science and environmental education center for visitors ages 5 to 12.

2050 Blowing Rock Hwy., Linville, 800-468-7325
grandfather.com

HIKE
GREAT SMOKY MOUNTAINS NATIONAL PARK

Straddling the border of North Carolina and Tennessee, Great Smoky Mountains National Park is America's most visited national park, welcoming about 13 million visitors annually.

It spans 521,085 acres and is home to more than 1,500 species of flowering plants, more than any other national park in North America. A bounty of wildlife resides here, too: almost 70 species of native fish, over 80 types of reptiles and amphibians, about 65 species of mammals, and close to 240 species of birds.

Over 850 miles of trails await exploration, whether you're seeking a leisurely stroll or a challenging trek. You can also overnight it in the park, with options ranging from developed campgrounds to backcountry sites for more adventurous campers.

nps.gov/grsm/index.htm

TIP

The main park entrance in North Carolina is just outside of Cherokee on US 441 North at the Oconaluftee Visitor Center, which is open year-round.

44

ROAD-TRIP
ALONG THE BLUE RIDGE PARKWAY

The Blue Ridge Parkway is often referred to as "America's Favorite Drive," and for good reason. Stretching 469 miles, it connects the Great Smoky Mountains National Park in North Carolina to Shenandoah National Park in Virginia, and it provides some of the most spectacular views America has to offer.

The parkway leads you along towering mountain ranges, dips down to river valleys, and winds through hilly pastures.

Along the drive through North Carolina, you'll pass through charming towns like Asheville, Boone, Blowing Rock, and Little Switzerland. Notable stops along the parkway in North Carolina include the Moses H. Cone Memorial Park, Linville Falls, and Mount Mitchell, the highest peak east of the Mississippi River.

Several overlooks along the parkway offer a chance to stretch your legs and soak in the scenery. Popular overlooks can be found along the Linn Cove Viaduct (Milepost 304.4), an engineering marvel that gracefully hugs Grandfather Mountain, and Cowee Mountain Overlook (Milepost 430.7), the perfect vantage point for watching the sun dip below the horizon, spreading a golden glimmer over the surrounding mountains.

The Blue Ridge Parkway also provides access to some of the nation's best hiking trails. The Lunch Rocks Trail (Milepost 382), the Black Balsam hike (Milepost 420.2), and the Hard Times Loop (Milepost 395) are a few to consider.

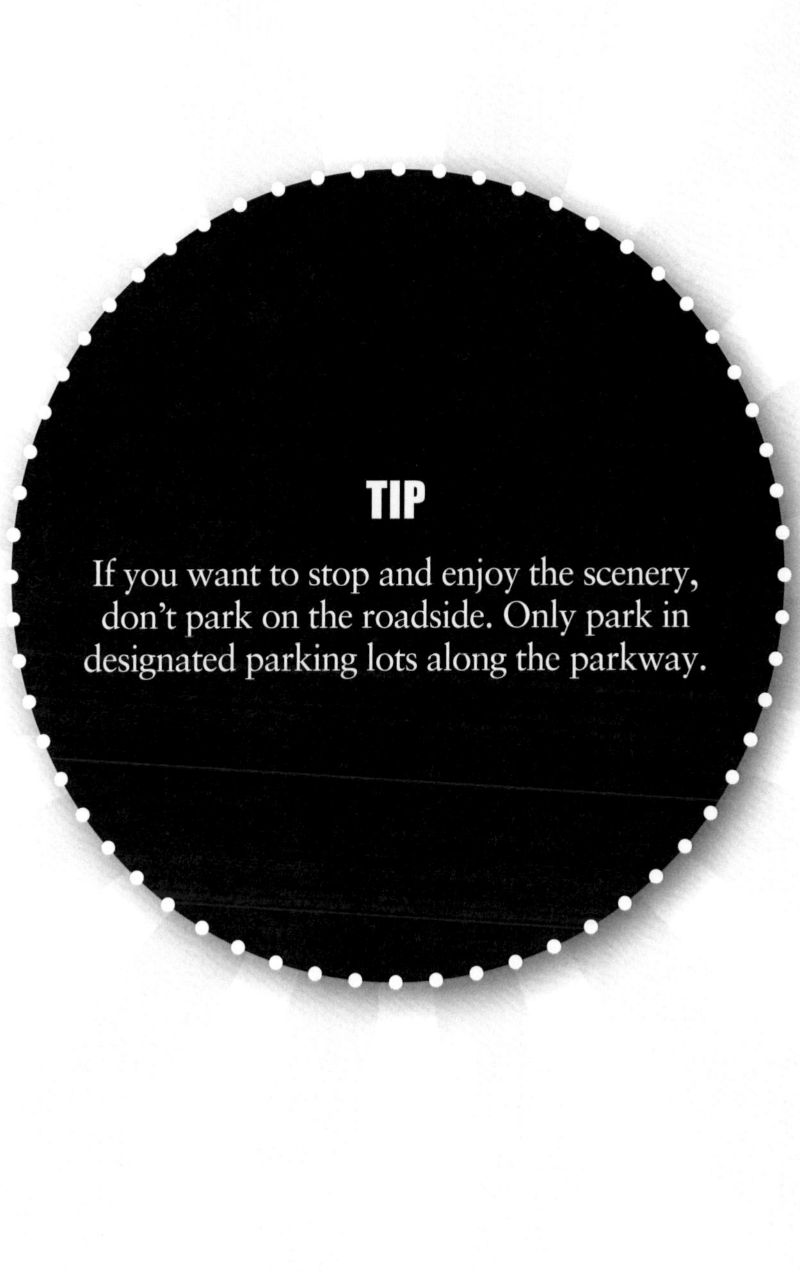

TIP

If you want to stop and enjoy the scenery, don't park on the roadside. Only park in designated parking lots along the parkway.

45

SEARCH
FOR LIGHTHOUSES

Embark on a coastal road trip in search of North Carolina's majestic lighthouses, symbols of the state's maritime heritage. Currituck Beach Lighthouse in Corolla is a striking red-brick lighthouse standing 162 feet tall. It's one of the few lighthouses to remain unpainted. Bodie Island Light Station is situated at the northern end of Cape Hatteras National Seashore. Unfortunately, the Bodie Island Double Keepers' Quarters (Visitor Center and Park Store) is closed indefinitely due to internal damage from a January 2025 fire. The outdoor areas remain open for visiting. Towering 210 feet high, Cape Hatteras Lighthouse is the tallest brick lighthouse in the US. The lighthouse was closed at the time of writing due to restoration work, but the Museum of the Sea and Park Store remain open. At the southern end of Cape Hatteras National Seashore, Ocracoke Lighthouse is the state's oldest lighthouse still in operation (constructed in 1823). Cape Lookout Lighthouse sits on Cape Lookout National Seashore. You can reach it only by boat or ferry, but the effort to get there is worth it. You'll be rewarded with unspoiled beaches and incredible views. North Carolina's oldest lighthouse, Bald Head Lighthouse or "Old Baldy," was built in 1817. The Smith Island Museum of History inside the keeper's cottage is a fantastic primer on Bald Head Island's history. The baby of North Carolina's lighthouses, Oak Island Lighthouse, went up in 1958. You can get to the top via a series of ship's ladders.

NORTH CAROLINA LIGHTHOUSES

Currituck Beach Lighthouse
1101 Corolla Village Rd., Corolla

Bodie Island Light Station
8210 Bodie Island Lighthouse Rd., Nags Head

Cape Hatteras Lighthouse
46379 Lighthouse Rd., Buxton

Ocracoke Lighthouse
360 Lighthouse Rd., Ocracoke

Cape Lookout Lighthouse
1800 Island Rd., Harkers Island

Old Baldy Lighthouse
101 Light House Wynd, Bald Head Island

Oak Island Lighthouse
300 Caswell Beach Rd., Oak Island

CHEER
FOR THE PANTHERS

Established in 1995, the Carolina Panthers bring electrifying NFL action to the Queen City of Charlotte. Home games take place at the Bank of America Stadium, an open-air arena that seats over 74,000 and offers fans panoramic views of the Charlotte skyline.

The Panthers reached the Super Bowl twice—in 2003 (losing to the Patriots) and in 2015 (falling to the Broncos). The team's signature "Keep Pounding" motto honors former player and coach Sam Mills, who inspired the team during his battle with cancer. The phrase resonated deeply with the team and fans, becoming a rallying cry for the Panthers. "Keep Pounding" symbolizes the team's and its community's determination to overcome challenges, embodying the spirit of never giving up.

Attending a Panthers game is more than just watching football; it's a full-day event with tailgating, fan festivities, and halftime shows. Stock up on fan favorites at the Panthers Team Store, which sells a solid selection of Panthers-related souvenirs.

800 S Mint St., Charlotte, 704-358-7480
panthers.com

47

STOP AND SMELL THE ROSES
AT BOTANICAL GARDENS

I could spend hours blissfully getting lost among lush gardens, babbling fountains, and bountiful fragrant flowers. Thankfully, North Carolina has no shortage of places to center yourself in nature. In Belmont, just outside Charlotte, the 380-acre Stowe (formerly Stowe Botanical Garden) is situated on the banks of Lake Wylie. Visitors can follow over eight miles of hiking trails. Kids can explore the new half-mile Adventure Trail, with outdoor play areas and a fully accessible Prairie Castle Playground. Spanning some 434 acres abundant with vibrant flower gardens, lush grounds, and forest trails, the North Carolina Arboretum in Asheville offers a lovely escape for the day. North Carolina Botanical Garden at the University of North Carolina at Chapel Hill is renowned for its carnivorous plant collection and its broad range of native plants, flowers, herbs, and mosses.

Stowe
6500 S New Hope Rd., Belmont
704-825-4490
dsbg.org

The North Carolina Arboretum
20 Frederick Law Olmsted Way
Asheville, 828-665-2492
ncarboretum.org

North Carolina Botanical Garden
100 Old Mason Farm Rd., Chapel Hill, 919-962-0522
ncbg.unc.edu

FOLLOW THE GLOW
OF BLUE GHOST FIREFLIES

For an other worldly experience, try to catch a glimpse of the blue ghost fireflies, a species of bioluminescent beetles found in the mountains of Western North Carolina.

What makes them so cool? Unlike other fireflies that flash on and off, blue ghost fireflies emit a steady, blue-green glow. This continuous luminescence creates an ethereal atmosphere in the forested landscapes they inhabit. According to Appalachian lore, fireflies are said to be ghosts of Confederate soldiers, as many of them died in the region where the fireflies emerge.

The best time to see the fireflies is from late May to early June, during their brief mating season. They're most active on warm, humid nights in dark, undisturbed wooded areas. Popular viewing spots include DuPont State Recreational Forest, Pisgah National Forest, and Cataloochee Valley.

DuPont State Recreational Forest
dupontforest.com

Pisgah National Forest
fs.usda.gov/recarea/nfsnc/recarea/?recid=48114

Cataloochee Valley
nps.gov/grsm/planyourvisit/cataloochee-balsam.htm

49

SCALE THE DUNES
AT JOCKEY'S RIDGE

Spanning over 400 acres, Jockey's Ridge State Park is home to the East Coast's tallest active sand dunes—some up to 60 feet high—offering an otherworldly landscape that continually changes due to the shifting sands.

The dunes are a popular spot for activities like hiking, kite flying, and sand boarding. Adventurous types can even go hang gliding here, as the soft sands provide a forgiving landing surface for both beginners and experts. The top of the dunes offers incredible views of the Outer Banks barrier islands, including the Atlantic Ocean to the east and Roanoke Sound to the west.

Make sure to stop by the well-curated visitor center, which is home to exhibits about the park's different habitats and the history of how the park came to be.

300 W Carolista Dr., Nags Head, 252-573-6108
ncparks.gov/state-parks/jockeys-ridge-state-park

CATCH THE BREEZE
AT THE BLOWING ROCK

An iconic rock formation in North Carolina's Blue Ridge Mountains, the Blowing Rock stands at 4,000 feet above sea level, overhanging Johns River Gorge 3,000 feet below. It's named for the strong winds that blow upward from the gorge below.

The legend of the Blowing Rock tells of a young Chickasaw maiden who, heartbroken by her lover's leap off the rock's precipice, prayed to the Great Spirit for his safe return. Her prayers were answered when a powerful wind blew him back up the rocky cliff, defying gravity. Blowing Rock opened as a tourist attraction in 1933 and has been declared the oldest travel attraction in North Carolina.

After checking out the literal Blowing Rock, head into town for a visit to Blowing Rock Art & History Museum, which showcases local art and historical exhibits. Refuel at the Speckled Trout, one of my favorite spots for fantastic Appalachian-inspired food.

Blowing Rock Market
990 Main St., Blowing Rock, 828-414-9322

Blowing Rock Art & History Museum
159 Ginny Stevens Ln., Blowing Rock, 828-295-9099
blowingrockmuseum.org

The Speckled Trout
922 Main St., Blowing Rock, 828-295-9819
thespeckledtrout.com

Blowing Rock Art & History Museum

Ava Gardner Museum
Credit Ava Gardner Museum

Carowinds
Credit Carowinds

Autumn at Oz
Credit Beech Mountain TDA

Mrs. Hanes' Moravian Cookies

NC Apple Festival Credit Tim Robison

Charlotte Regional Farmers Market

North Carolina Museum of Art

Ocean Isle Beach Canals
Credit North Carolina's
Brunswick Islands

Azalea Festival Parade
Credit Azalea Festival

Richard Petty Museum
Credit HeartofNorthCarolina.com

Seagrove Pottery
Credit HeartofNorthCarolina.com

Sullenberger Aviation Museum

Sunset in Southport
Credit North Carolina's Brunswick Islands

Tweetsie Railroad
Credit Tweetsie Railroad

Chimney Rock

51

CHASE CASCADES
IN THE LAND OF THE WATERFALLS

North Carolina is home to hundreds of waterfalls. More than 250 of them are in Transylvania County's Brevard area alone, earning it the title "Land of the Waterfalls." Here are a few—in Brevard and beyond—to get you going.

Head to the Highlands area for a walk behind the cascading water of Dry Falls without getting wet. Also, the delicate cascade of Bridal Veil Falls resembles a bride's veil. Additionally, enjoy a handful of scenic stops along a two-mile round-trip hike to reach Glen Falls, a gorgeous triple waterfall. Within Pisgah National Forest, look for a kaleidoscope of colors at Rainbow Falls.

Chimney Rock State Park's towering 404-foot Hickory Nut Falls was featured in the blockbuster movie *The Last of the Mohicans*. Its powerful rush and misty spray create an amazing spectacle.

Deep in the Nantahala National Forest near the Georgia state line, Secret Falls requires a short hike to reach a gorgeous 50-foot waterfall that cascades into a serene pool.

TIP

Explore Brevard offers a comprehensive interactive map for all your waterfall-chasing adventures in Transylvania County. You'll find it at explorebrevard.com/naturally-rooted/land-of-waterfalls.

52

GLIDE DOWN AND COOL OFF
AT SLIDING ROCK

While you're chasing waterfalls in Transylvania County, make sure to add Sliding Rock to your list of stops.

Located in the Pisgah National Forest, this smooth rock formation was shaped over time by the flowing waters of Looking Glass Creek, making the perfect natural waterslide. Prepare yourself for a thrilling 60-foot descent down a sloping granite boulder into an eight-foot-deep pool. This beloved summer destination attracts thousands of visitors who brave the chilly 50-to-60-degree mountain water for an exhilarating ride.

The US Forest Service maintains the site with lifeguards, observation decks, changing rooms, and restrooms from Memorial Day through Labor Day. Ample parking and picnic spots are available in the surrounding area.

Make sure to wear sturdy water shoes and durable swimwear—the rock can be rough on clothing. Arrive early in the day to avoid crowds, especially on hot summer weekends. The site is particularly magical in the early morning when mist rises from the forest and the water sparkles in the sunlight.

7851 Pisgah Hwy., Pisgah Forest, 828-577-4910
fs.usda.gov/recarea/nfsnc/recarea/?recid=48156

SHOOT FOR THE STARS

AT MAYLAND EARTH TO SKY PARK

In Burnsville, the Mayland Earth to Sky Park features a remarkable Bare Dark Sky Observatory that draws stargazers from around the world.

The site's minimal light pollution earned it the coveted International Dark Sky Park designation, making it one of the few certified dark sky locations in the southeastern United States. The observatory is perched at an elevation of 2,736 feet and houses a 34-inch Newtonian telescope, providing stunning views of planets, star clusters, and distant galaxies.

Public viewing nights, guided tours and astronomy programs, and special events during meteor showers and other astronomical phenomena are other reasons to visit.

The Glenn & Carol Arthur Planetarium also hosts traditional astronomy shows and other STEM educational programs.

66 Energy Exchange Dr., Burnsville, 828-470-7584
mayland.edu/foundation/foundation-events/earth-to-sky-observatory

TIP

Viewing night sessions often sell out, so advance reservations are recommended.

54

TREK ALONG
THE APPALACHIAN TRAIL

A legendary hiking route, the Appalachian Trail stretches approximately 2,190 miles across the eastern United States, from Springer Mountain in Georgia to Mount Katahdin in Maine. It is one of the longest continuously marked footpaths in the world, traversing 14 states and offering a diverse range of landscapes, from dense forests to awe-inspiring mountain vistas.

The North Carolina section of the Appalachian Trail is around 220 miles, much of which is along the North Carolina and Tennessee border. This section includes some of the trail's most scenic and challenging terrains, such as the Great Smoky Mountains National Park and the majestic peaks of the Blue Ridge Mountains. Hikers can explore iconic landmarks such as Max Patch, known for its stunning panoramic views, and the 6,643-foot Kuwohi, formerly called Clingmans Dome, the highest mountain on the Appalachian Trail.

It typically takes about three to four weeks to hike the North Carolina portion of the Appalachian Trail. However, that estimate depends on the hiker's fitness level, experience, and the time of year. This section provides an unforgettable journey through the heart of the Appalachian wilderness, offering a mix of natural beauty and rugged adventure. The trail connects with numerous side trails and camping areas, making it accessible for both day hikers and long-distance backpackers.

appalachiantrail.org

55

HELP SAVE THE TURTLES
IN SURF CITY

The Karen Beasley Sea Turtle Rescue and Rehabilitation Center is a must for nature lovers and wildlife enthusiasts visiting Surf City. The nonprofit organization is dedicated to rescuing, rehabilitating, and releasing injured or sick sea turtles. It also works tirelessly to protect sea turtle habitats, monitor nests, and educate the public about marine conservation.

Guided tours provide insight into the world of sea turtles, their life cycles, and the challenges they face, such as pollution, boat strikes, and climate change. Observe turtles in rehabilitation tanks and hear inspiring stories of their recovery and release back into the wild.

302 Tortuga Ln., Surf City, 910-329-0222
seaturtlehospital.org

TIP

Tours require a ticket, which you must reserve in advance online. Available spots sell out daily, so plan your visit well in advance.

56

GO DEEP
IN LINVILLE CAVERNS

North Carolina's only active limestone caverns open to visitors, Linville Caverns is a cool, ethereal wonderland.

The caverns were discovered in 1822 by fishermen puzzled by what appeared to be trout swimming through the mountain. The fish led them to an opening that revealed an extensive cave system within Humpback Mountain, formed over millions of years by slowly moving groundwater dissolving the limestone.

Captivating visitors since opening to the public in 1937, Linville Caverns have been owned by the same family since 1940. Guided tours reveal illuminated chambers showcasing distinctive formations of stalactites, stalagmites, and flowing underground streams where blind trout still swim. The most dramatic formation is the "Bottomless Pool," where crystal-clear waters create mesmerizing reflections.

The caverns maintain a constant 52-degree temperature year-round, making them a refreshing summer destination and a cozy winter retreat. Fall and winter visitors might spy tricolored and little brown bats, as the caverns serve as a hibernation site for them.

Located just off US 221 near Marion, the caverns offer easily accessible parking and a gift shop.

19929 US-221, Marion, 828-756-4171
linvillecaverns.com

TIP

From March through November, Linville Caverns are open Thursday through Monday from 9 a.m. to 6 p.m. From December through February, the caverns are open on weekends from 9 a.m. to 4:30 p.m. Tours are limited to 15 people at a time and are first come, first served at the caverns.

57

PREDICT THE WEATHER
AT THE WOOLLY WORM FESTIVAL

Pennsylvania may have Punxsutawney Phil, but North Carolina has its own way to predict the weather, thanks to Merriweather the Woolly Worm.

Held in October each year, the Woolly Worm Festival in Banner Elk has captured the hearts of locals and visitors since its inception in 1978. Attracting around 20,000 attendees annually, this festival is centered around the woolly worm, a caterpillar believed to predict the severity of the upcoming winter based on its black and brown bands.

The festival features the famous Woolly Worm Races, where competitors race their woolly worms up a three-foot string. The winner's worm is said to forecast the winter weather.

Beyond the races, visitors can enjoy a variety of activities, including live entertainment, craft vendors showcasing handmade goods, food stalls offering local cuisine, and a children's play area with games and rides. The festival also hosts a parade and a costume contest, adding to the festive atmosphere. This family-friendly event provides a vibrant mix of tradition, fun, and community spirit, making it a standout attraction in the region.

185 Azalea Cir., Banner Elk, 828-898-5605
woollyworm.com

OTHER NORTH CAROLINA FESTIVALS

North Carolina Azalea Festival

Historic downtown Wilmington blooms bright each spring when the North Carolina Azalea Festival is in full swing. The festival began in 1948 and has grown into one of the state's most beloved traditions, attracting nearly 300,000 visitors each year.

5725 Oleander Dr., Wilmington, 910-794-4650
ncazaleafestival.org

Balloonfest

Launched in 1978 and held in Statesville every third weekend in October, Carolina BalloonFest is the country's second-longest-running hot air balloon event.

531 Old Airport Rd., Statesville, 888-803-4464
carolinaballoonfest.com

Charlotte Shout!

This festival celebrates the city's art, culture, and community. It features more than 200 events, and attractions in various venues and locations across Uptown, Charlotte.

charlotteshout.com

Swansboro Mullet Festival

Pay homage to the small, bony fish found in Eastern North Carolina waters. This fall festival began in 1954 and features local vendors, live music, and other activities.

swansborofestivals.com/mullet-festival

WATCH WILD HORSES
ROAM FREE

The wild horses of Corolla and Shackleford Banks are a captivating sight. How they got here is a mystery, but they are believed to be descendants of Spanish mustangs that arrived in the area as early as the 16th century.

See the Corolla Wild Horses as part of a guided tour in an off-road vehicle through the sandy terrain of the Currituck National Wildlife Refuge, where the horses roam freely.

Beaufort's Cape Lookout National Seashore is home to the Shackleford Banks horses. It's accessible only by boat, and guided tours here often include ferry rides and the opportunity to explore the island on foot.

Also in Beaufort, the Rachel Carson Reserve is home to about 35 feral horses introduced to the site by a local physician in the 1940s. Visitors can view the horses by boat, on a self-guided hike through the reserve, or via a local ecotour company.

Corolla Wild Horses
corollawildhorses.com

Shackleford Wild Horses
nps.gov/calo/learn/nature/horses.htm

Rachel Carson Reserve
fws.gov/refuge/rachel-carson

59

FLIP AND BUMP
AT A PINBALL MUSEUM

You don't have to be a pinball wizard to kick it old school at one of Asheville's most distinct attractions. Part arcade, part museum, the Asheville Pinball Museum features more than 40 vintage pinball machines and 40 classic video games, including Donkey Kong, PacMan, and Q-bert.

You can watch for free, and one price gets you in to play—no quarters needed! Adults pay $17, and children 10 and under play for $12. If you work up an appetite (or thirst), they also offer snacks, drinks, and beer. History buffs will appreciate the museum's location. It's housed in the city's Battery Park Hotel Building, which is listed on the National Register of Historic Places.

Hendersonville is home to Asheville Pinball Museum's sister venue, Appalachian Pinball Museum. As with the Asheville location, a variety of both vintage and contemporary pinball machines, plus classic arcade games, await players.

Asheville Pinball Museum
1 Battle Square, Ste. 1B, Asheville, 828-776-5671
pinball.ashevillepinball.com

Appalachian Pinball Museum
538 N Main St., Hendersonville, 828-702-9277
facebook.com/pinballplayers

ZIP THROUGH THE WOODS
ON AN ALPINE COASTER

The North Carolina mountains provide a bounty of outdoor experiences, but few match the exhilaration of whipping through the trees coaster-style. In Banner Elk, you can do just that.

Climb in a car and whiz along the 3,160-foot track at Wilderness Run Alpine Coaster, the first of its kind in North Carolina. Its track features a series of waves, several twists and turns, and three circular loops (not the upside down kind!). The coaster can reach speeds up to 27 mph. However, riders control the speed, so you can take it slower if you want. Note that anyone over 3 years old and at least 38 inches tall can ride, but you must be at least 16 to drive it.

Once you've tested your mettle on the coaster, try your skills in the air at the Wilderness Run Adventure Course, located next door. Climb through a series of 28 obstacles of ropes, planks, nets, and swinging bridges. Smaller climbers will dig the children's course. Ideal for adventurers from ages 2 to 5, it features bridges, platforms, and netted tubes.

3265 Tynecastle Hwy., Banner Elk, 828-898-7866
wildernessrunalpinecoaster.com

61

VISIT A GOLF MECCA
AT PINEHURST

Nestled in the Sandhills of North Carolina, Pinehurst Resort is a legendary destination for golf enthusiasts and leisure travelers alike. Established in 1895 by James Walker Tufts, Pinehurst was originally conceived as a health retreat.

Over the years, it evolved into a world-renowned resort, celebrated for its exceptional golf courses and Southern charm. Its crown jewel, Pinehurst No. 2, designed by Donald Ross in 1907, has hosted numerous prestigious tournaments, including the US Open. (The US Women's Open will return to Pinehurst in 2029.)

Beyond golf, the resort boasts luxurious accommodations, a full-service spa, and diverse dining options. The sprawling grounds are meticulously maintained, offering picturesque walking paths and tranquil settings.

Adjacent to the resort, Pinehurst Village enchants visitors with its New England–inspired architecture, quaint shops, and inviting cafés. It earned a National Historic Landmark designation in 1996.

TIP

Pop into the Villager Deli, a local favorite for breakfast and lunch since it opened in 1982. Chow down on a variety of sandwiches, salads, burgers, and other tasty items. Whatever you order, make sure to save room for a slice of homemade Chocolate Chess Pie.

62

EXPLORE
RACING HISTORY

North Carolina's NASCAR roots run deep, tracing back to the Prohibition era when local moonshiners modified their cars to outrun law enforcement. These souped-up vehicles eventually led to organized races, which began in 1948, with the first NASCAR race in Daytona Beach, Florida.

Since 1960, Concord's Charlotte Motor Speedway has been a cornerstone of this legacy. The speedway hosts major NASCAR events like the Coca-Cola 600 and the NASCAR All-Star Race, drawing massive crowds and offering an exhilarating experience for fans.

Downtown Charlotte is where you'll find the NASCAR Hall of Fame, which celebrates racing legends with exhibits showcasing cars, memorabilia, and interactive displays.

Head to Randalman for a tour of the Petty Museum, which honors the "King of NASCAR," Richard Petty. With 200 race wins that spanned three decades, Petty is the NASCAR's most decorated driver. The museum celebrates his remarkable career with family heirlooms, cars, NASCAR memorabilia, and other items.

In Wilkesboro you'll find North Wilkesboro Speedway, a pillar of NASCAR since its earliest days, hosting its first race in 1947—before NASCAR even officially formed. The speedway closed in the 1990s. However, it encountered a renaissance thanks to a committed racing community and dedicated fans and reopened in 2022.

NORTH CAROLINA NASCAR VENUES

Charlotte Motor Speedway

5555 Concord Pkwy. S, Concord
800-455-3267
charlottemotorspeedway.com

NASCAR Hall of Fame

400 E Martin Luther King Jr. Blvd., Charlotte
704-654-4400
nascarhall.com

Petty Museum

309 Branson Mill Rd., Randleman
336-495-1143
richardpettymuseum.com

North Wilkesboro Speedway

381 Speedway Ln., North Wilkesboro
336-844-4735
northwilkesborospeedway.com

N.C. Transportation Museum

CULTURE AND HISTORY

63

LEARN THE STORIES OF FREEDOM
AT THE WASHINGTON WATERFRONT UNDERGROUND RAILROAD MUSEUM

Many rivers and canals in North Carolina provided escape routes for enslaved people seeking freedom. One of the state's most prominent freedom roads, Pamlico River flows into the coastal town of Washington, placing it in the heart of the Underground Railroad.

The Washington Waterfront Underground Railroad Museum offers a compelling glimpse into the region's history with the Underground Railroad. The museum is housed in a restored Seaboard Coastline Railroad caboose, symbolizing the journey and transportation routes used by freedom seekers. At about 500 square feet, it's a modest but powerful space. However, it provides an educational and emotional experience that highlights this significant chapter in American history.

Stories of African Americans who sought freedom are told through exhibits, including artifacts, photographs, and narratives detailing the perilous journeys of escaping slaves and the network of people who assisted them. The museum is open on Thursdays through Sundays from 11 a.m. to 4 p.m.

Corner of Main and Gladden St., Washington, 609-444-8974
facebook.com/WashingtonNCfreedomseeking

64

DISCOVER THE WHEELS
THROUGH TIME MUSEUM

If you're visiting North Carolina with a motorcycle enthusiast, make your way to the Wheels Through Time Museum in Maggie Valley.

Founded by Dale Walksler in 1993, the museum houses a remarkable collection of more than 300 rare and vintage American motorcycles, thousands of photographs, historic memorabilia, and other artifacts. The exhibits cover a wide range of transportation history, with a focus on the evolution of the American motorcycle industry.

Visitors can view motorcycles from early pioneers like Harley-Davidson, Indian, and Excelsior, plus rare models dating back to the early 1900s. Motorcycle buffs will awe at displays that showcase mechanical innovations, designs, and craftsmanship that shaped the motorcycle industry. Interactive displays and live demonstrations bring the exhibits to life, with mechanics often on hand to restore and repair vintage bikes.

62 Vintage Ln., Maggie Valley, 828-926-6266
wheelsthroughtime.com

TIP

The museum closes during the winter months, so plan your visit accordingly.

65

DIVE INTO
THE GRAVEYARD OF THE ATLANTIC MUSEUM

More than 5,000 ships rest in the waters off the Outer Banks. Shifting sandbars, treacherous currents, navigational error, piracy, and war all contributed to their demise, earning the area the moniker "Graveyard of the Atlantic."

Scuba divers can explore many of the wrecks, including three World War II–era U-boats, the luxury liner Proteus that sank in 1918, and several vessels purposely sunk to create an artificial reef for marine life. If you prefer to stay on land but can't get enough maritime history, the Graveyard of the Atlantic Museum is for you. It's just about 10 miles southwest of Cape Hatteras Lighthouse.

The museum's striking design mirrors the curves and elements of seafaring vessels. This 7,800-square-foot museum might not take up much real estate, but it packs a significant historical punch. It houses more than 1,500 artifacts, offering visitors a deep dive into the region's nautical past.

Exhibits include artifacts from shipwrecks dating back to the 16th century, salvaged items from the infamous USS Monitor and Queen Anne's Revenge, and displays on piracy, including relics associated with Blackbeard. Interactive displays like the periscope exhibit bring compelling maritime tales to life.

59200 Museum Dr., Hatteras, 252-986-0720
graveyardoftheatlantic.com

SPEND THE NIGHT
IN HISTORIC GRAYLYN ESTATE

You don't need to venture across the pond for a dreamy stay in a European-style castle. Just head to Winston-Salem and check into Graylyn Estate.

The enchanting 55-acre property began in 1932 as the home of Bowman Gray, a prominent tobacco executive, and his wife, Nathalie. At the time it was constructed, Graylyn Estate was the state's second-largest private home (behind Asheville's Biltmore Estate).

Nathalie Gray's passion for travel is evident in every nook and cranny, from the 17th-century hand-carved paneling from the Hotel d'Estrades in Paris to the estate's Persian Card Room, where you'll find some of the world's oldest examples of Syrian art. Original features like hand-wrought ironwork, imported tiles, and custom stonework showcase the craftsmanship of the era. Enjoy a delectable meal in the main dining room and sample after-dinner cocktails fireside in the cozy Grille Room downstairs.

1900 Reynolda Rd., Winston-Salem, 336-758-2425
graylyn.com

TIP

Spring for a butler tour, which you can reserve online when you book your stay. The roughly hour-and-a-half tour offers fascinating details about the property's history.

SEE THE "MIRACLE ON THE HUDSON" AND MORE AT THE SULLENBERGER AVIATION MUSEUM

The event was arguably one of the most compelling aviation stories in recent history. On January 15, 2009, US Airways Flight 1549 was headed to Charlotte when it struck a flock of birds and lost engine power over New York City. Pilots Capt. Chesley "Sully" Sullenberger and Jeffrey Skiles successfully landed the disabled plane in the Hudson River. All 155 people on board survived, and the flight was dubbed the "Miracle on the Hudson."

The Sullenberger Aviation Museum now holds the iconic aircraft, plus a display of items from passengers and crew members on board. A video takes visitors through the events of that day and includes the cockpit recording of the incident and news reports.

The three-building campus also houses more than 40 aircraft and an extensive collection of artifacts that trace aviation history and innovation. From the Aviation Plaza, watch the planes take off from Charlotte Douglas International Airport.

4108 Minuteman Way, Charlotte, 704-997-3770
sullenbergeraviation.org

68

TOUR THE HAMLET DEPOT & MUSEUMS

History buffs and train lovers will get their fill at the Hamlet Depot & Museums, site of the oldest train station in North Carolina.

Dating back to 1900, the depot is a classic example of Queen Anne–style architecture and is listed on the National Register of Historic Places. It served as a vital hub for the Seaboard Air Line Railroad, playing a significant role in the development of the region.

The museum complex includes the historic depot, a locomotive, a caboose, and several other exhibits that showcase the rich history of railroads in the area. Visitors can explore a variety of artifacts, photographs, and interactive displays that bring the era of train travel to life. The museum also highlights the cultural and economic impact of the railroads on the town of Hamlet and surrounding communities.

It's free to tour the Hamlet Depot & Museums, making it an accessible and educational experience for all ages.

2 Main St., Hamlet, 910-582-0603
hamlethistoricdepot.org

69

STROLL THROUGH HISTORY
IN OLD SALEM

The beautifully preserved historic district of Old Salem offers a glimpse into early American life. It was established in 1766 by the Moravians, a Protestant religious group from Europe seeking religious freedom.

Some buildings require a ticket to enter, which you can purchase at the Old Salem Visitor Center before you begin exploring.

Visit the Single Brothers' House, constructed in 1769. It served as a communal living space for unmarried men and now functions as a museum illustrating their trades and daily lives. Winkler Bakery, one of America's oldest continuously operated bakeries, offers mouthwatering Moravian sugar cakes and Lovefeast buns.

The Moravian Candle Tea at Old Salem, a local tradition since 1929 is a memorable way to celebrate Christmas. Costumed guides lead guests on a tour of the Single Brothers' House, which includes caroling and traditional beeswax candle-making demonstrations. A highlight is a warm mug of sweet Moravian coffee with a piece of fresh-baked Moravian sugar cake.

900 Old Salem Rd., Winston-Salem, 336-721-7350
oldsalem.org

TIP

Candle Tea is sponsored by the Home Moravian Church Women's Fellowship. You can purchase tickets through the Home Moravian Church website at homemoravian.org/our-ministries.

70

VISIT GREEN BOOK LEGACY SITES

The Green Book Legacy Sites in North Carolina honor the history and resilience of African Americans during segregation. Published from 1936 to 1966, the Green Book was a guide for African American travelers, listing safe places to stay, eat, and visit in a segregated America.

Hundreds of North Carolina businesses were listed in the Green Book, and some of them are still open today. Among them include the Pauli Murray House in Durham, which celebrates the life of Pauli Murray, a civil rights activist and cofounder of the National Organization for Women.

The International Civil Rights Center & Museum in Greensboro, housed in the former Woolworth's building, commemorates the 1960 sit-ins that helped ignite the Civil Rights Movement. Additionally, Greensboro's Historic Magnolia House served as a Green Book–listed hotel, offering lodging to African American travelers during segregation.

The Thomas Day House and Union Tavern in Milton was the home and workshop of Thomas Day, a free Black furniture maker in the 19th century. Currituck County's Historic Jarvisburg Colored School Museum preserves one of North Carolina's first schools for African American children.

NORTH CAROLINA GREEN BOOK SITES

International Civil Rights Center & Museum

134 S Elm St., Greensboro, 336-274-9199
sitinmovement.org

The Historic Magnolia House

442 Gorrell St., Greensboro, 336-617-3382
thehistoricmagnoliahouse.org

Pauli Murray Center for History and Social Justice

906 Carroll St., Durham, 919-229-9013
paulimurraycenter.com

Thomas Day State Historic Site

148 Broad St., Milton, 336-234-0030
facebook.com/thomasdayhouse

Historic Jarvisburg Colored School Museum

7302 Caratoke Hwy., Jarvisburg, 252-491-2409
hjcschool.org

71

TAKE FLIGHT
AT THE WRIGHT BROTHERS NATIONAL MEMORIAL

The Wright Brothers National Memorial in Kill Devil Hills commemorates the first successful powered flights by Orville and Wilbur Wright in December 1903. The memorial features a 60-foot granite monument atop Kill Devil Hill, honoring the Wright brothers' pioneering achievements.

Kitty Hawk was the ideal environment for their flight experiments. Its strong winds provided good lift for the aircraft, and the sand provided a soft landing.

Visitors can explore the reconstructed camp buildings, including the brothers' living quarters and 1903 hangar. The site also includes the First Flight Boulder, marking the takeoff point of the first flight, and the Flight Path Walkway, which traces the paths of the first four flights. The visitor center houses a museum with original artifacts, photographs, and exhibits detailing the Wright brothers' experiments and the impact of their success on the world.

1000 N Croatan Hwy., Kill Devil Hills, 252-473-2111
nps.gov/wrbr/index.htm

MAN YOUR STATIONS
ON THE BATTLESHIP *NORTH CAROLINA*

The Battleship *North Carolina*, a World War II icon, is moored in Wilmington. Commissioned in 1941, it played a pivotal role in the Pacific Theater, earning 15 battle stars, the most of any American battleship. Decommissioned in 1947, the battleship opened as a museum in 1962.

Visitors can explore nine levels of the ship, including the engine room, crew's quarters, and massive gun turrets. The self-guided tour provides an immersive experience, enhanced by interactive exhibits and historical artifacts.

Throughout the year, the battleship hosts special events such as Memorial Day and Veterans Day ceremonies, as well as educational programs and reenactments. If ghost hunting is your thing, book an after-hours paranormal tour aboard the ship available through a handful of tour companies.

1 Battleship Rd. NE, Wilmington, 910-399-9100
battleshipnc.com

CELEBRATE THE NORTH CAROLINA CHINESE LANTERN FESTIVAL

The North Carolina Chinese Lantern Festival in Cary is an enchanting annual event that first began in 2015. Organized by Tianyu Arts & Culture, Inc., this dazzling festival typically runs from mid-November to mid-January. It takes place at Koka Booth Amphitheatre, a beautiful outdoor venue situated amid pine trees and a scenic lake.

Each year, the festival showcases more than 40 larger-than-life lantern displays, meticulously handcrafted by skilled Chinese artisans. These vibrant displays, illuminated at night, depict a variety of themes, including animals, flowers, and Chinese folklore, creating a mesmerizing visual experience for visitors of all ages.

Alongside the enchanting lanterns, attendees can enjoy cultural performances such as traditional Chinese dance, music, and acrobatics. Food options are plentiful, ranging from the Crescent Cafe to food trucks on weekends. They serve a variety of Asian cuisine, including spring rolls, ramen, dumplings, and more.

8003 Regency Pkwy., Cary, 919-462-2025
facebook.com/NCChineseLanternFestival

EXPERIENCE
THE INTERNATIONAL CIVIL RIGHTS CENTER & MUSEUM

The International Civil Rights Center & Museum in Greensboro stands as a pivotal institution dedicated to the history and legacy of the Civil Rights Movement.

The museum occupies the former F.W. Woolworth building, site of one of the most significant moments in civil rights history. Here, on February 1, 1960, four Black college students from North Carolina Agricultural and Technical State University staged a peaceful sit-in at the Whites-only lunch counter.

The Woolworth sit-in was a substantial triumph for the Civil Rights Movement, showing that nonviolent protests could be effective in challenging discrimination and segregation. The sit-in also helped amplify support for civil rights, inspiring other activists to take similar actions.

A variety of exhibits and programs tell the story of the Civil Rights Movement, from the early days of slavery to the modern-day fight for equality. Notably, the original lunch counter remains preserved, allowing guests to connect directly with this significant piece of history. The museum also features reenactments, artifacts, plus educational displays that provide a comprehensive understanding of the fight for civil and human rights.

134 S Elm St., Greensboro, 336-274-9199
sitinmovement.org

75

TAKE A TOUR
OF THE NORTH CAROLINA TRANSPORTATION MUSEUM

The North Carolina Transportation Museum, located in Spencer, opened its doors in 1983. Housed in the former Southern Railway Spencer Shops, this museum preserves and showcases the rich transportation history of North Carolina. Spencer, a town deeply tied to the railway industry, became a vital hub in the early 20th century, with the Spencer Shops serving as one of the Southeast's largest locomotive repair facilities.

The museum spans over 60 acres and offers a fascinating glimpse into the evolution of transportation. Its exhibits include an impressive collection of locomotives, railcars, automobiles, and airplanes. Notable artifacts include historic steam and diesel locomotives, passenger cars, and cabooses. Visitors can also explore vintage automobiles and airplanes, providing a comprehensive view of transportation history beyond the railways.

The museum also features a train ride experience, allowing visitors to enjoy a ride on historic railcars (the last ride is at 2 p.m.).

1 Samuel Spencer Dr., Spencer, 704-636-2889
nctransportationmuseum.org

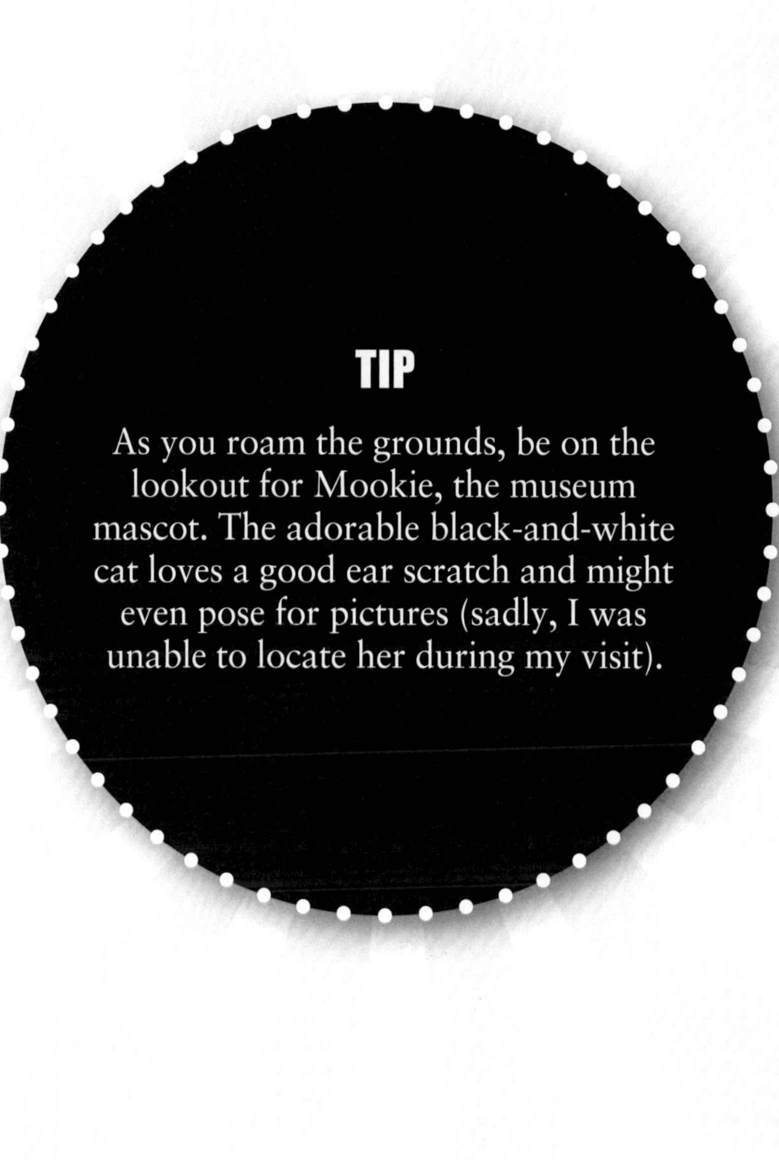

TIP

As you roam the grounds, be on the lookout for Mookie, the museum mascot. The adorable black-and-white cat loves a good ear scratch and might even pose for pictures (sadly, I was unable to locate her during my visit).

76

RETRACE
BLACKBEARD'S FOOTSTEPS

The infamous pirate Blackbeard knew many harbors, but North Carolina was his true home. Born Edward Teach (or possibly Thatch), Blackbeard served as a privateer for England in Queen Anne's War, turning to piracy at war's end in 1713. He's believed to have come to North Carolina around 1717. While he had many hideouts and sailed throughout the Caribbean and Atlantic, he established a strong presence in North Carolina, particularly in the town of Bath.

Begin your Blackbeard journey in Beaufort. Back in the day, it was known as a pirate haven, with Blackbeard and his crew frequenting the area. Here you'll want to explore the North Carolina Maritime Museum, which houses artifacts from his ship Queen Anne's Revenge, including cannons, grenades, beads, and belt buckles. The site of the wreck is under about 20 feet of water just offshore from Fort Macon State Park in Atlantic Beach. Museum exhibits tell the story of Blackbeard's life and piracy along the Atlantic. In Beaufort, take a stroll past the historic Hammock House, where Blackbeard is believed to have stayed when the house was an inn.

Head to Bath and explore the town where Blackbeard briefly attempted a life of legitimacy. He received a pardon from Governor Charles Eden, settled there, and even married before returning to piracy. Tour the historic Van der Veer House, which has a room dedicated to Blackbeard that includes a graphite vase—rumored to be his money pot.

Blackbeard met his demise on Ocracoke Island in 1718. His last stand occurred at Teach's Hole, an inlet where British naval forces killed him in battle. If you plan to overnight it in Ocracoke, book a room at Blackbeard's Lodge, a popular vacation destination since 1936.

North Carolina Maritime Museums
315 Front St., Beaufort
252-504-7740
ncmaritimemuseumbeaufort.com

Blackbeard's Lodge
111 Back Rd., Ocracoke
252-928-3421
blackbeardslodge.com

VISIT
NORTH CAROLINA'S FIRST TOWN

Bath, North Carolina, the state's first incorporated town, is a captivating destination where history and natural beauty intertwine. Established in 1705, this small waterfront community played a pivotal role in North Carolina's colonial past, serving as the first port of entry and a center for early trade.

Visit Historic Bath, where 18th-century structures like the Palmer-Marsh House and Bonner House transport guests to the colonial era. These preserved homes offer guided tours and insights into the daily lives of Bath's early settlers. Bath is also home to St. Thomas Episcopal Church. Built in 1734, it's the oldest church in North Carolina.

Bath's connection to Edward Teach, better known as the notorious pirate Blackbeard, adds a layer of intrigue. Blackbeard arrived in Bath in 1718 and was offered a pardon by the town's colonial governor Charles Eden (if he promised to cease his pirate shenanigans). Blackbeard made good on his word—for a little while, at least. He moved on to Ocracoke, where he was killed during a bloody battle with a British navy force sent from Virginia.

100 S Harding St., Bath, 252-741-6030
historicsites.nc.gov/all-sites/historic-bath

PAN FOR GOLD
AT REED GOLD MINE

Many associate gold with the state of California thanks to the 1848 discovery of the precious metal at Sutter's Mill. That event launched the California Gold Rush, the largest migration in the nation's history. However, the first documented gold find in the United States actually occurred nearly 50 years earlier on the opposite side of the country, in Midland, North Carolina.

In 1799, 12-year-old Conrad Reed found a 17-pound gold nugget in a creek on his family's modest farm. Word of the discovery later drew gold hunters by the droves. In its heyday, gold mining in North Carolina was second only to farming, with over $1 million recovered each year. The state led the nation in gold production until 1848 when all eyes looked to California.

Dig deeper into North Carolina's gold history at the Reed Gold Mine, on the site where young Conrad fished his nugget from the creek. The state historic site is the nation's largest open-pit mine and North Carolina's only active gold mine. The mine features mine tunnels where visitors can see the veins of white quartz where the gold was found, as well as exhibits showcasing the area's mining history.

9621 Reed Mine Rd., Midland, 704-721-4653
historicsites.nc.gov/all-sites/reed-gold-mine

79

FOLLOW THE ASHEVILLE BLACK CULTURAL HERITAGE TRAIL

The Asheville Black Cultural Heritage Trail, established in 2022, offers a profound exploration of Asheville's rich African American history. Trail markers guide you to significant landmarks that played pivotal roles in the Black community's cultural, social, and economic development.

The trail takes you through three areas of Asheville: downtown, southside, and the River Area. Key stops include the YMI Cultural Center, one of the oldest African American institutions in the country, and the historic Stephens-Lee High School, known as the "Castle on the Hill," which was a cornerstone for Black education in Asheville.

Other notable landmarks include the Southside neighborhood, the Eagle Street area, and the groundbreaking achievements of local Black entrepreneurs and civic leaders. The trail typically takes about two to three hours to complete, depending on your pace and how much time you spend at each stop. This enriching experience offers visitors a deeper understanding of Asheville's African American legacy.

bcht.exploreasheville.com/follow-the-trail

VISIT THE BILLY GRAHAM LIBRARY

Opened in 2007, the Billy Graham Library in Charlotte is dedicated to the life and ministry of the renowned evangelist Billy Graham. The library offers a journey through the history of Graham's influential work and Christian ministry.

Visitors can explore a range of exhibits, including multimedia presentations, memorabilia from Graham's global evangelistic crusades, and personal artifacts that provide insight into his life and mission. One of the highlights is the re-created Graham family home, offering a glimpse into his humble beginnings. The Journey of Faith tour guides visitors through interactive displays that recount Graham's message of hope and faith, showcasing his impact on millions worldwide.

The library is open Mondays through Saturdays from 9:30 a.m. to 5 p.m., except select holidays. Admission is free.

4330 Westmont Dr., Charlotte, 704-401-3200
billygrahamlibrary.org

TIP

If you worked up an appetite during your tour, grab a bite at the Graham Brothers Dairy Bar. Nosh on a chicken salad sandwich or Billy Frank hot dog. Craving a sweet treat? Order an ice cream sandwich or a soft-serve cone.

81

EXPLORE NATIVE AMERICAN CULTURE
IN CHEROKEE

Situated in the Great Smoky Mountains, Cherokee is home to the Eastern Band of Cherokee Indians, and a cultural treasure for the curious traveler. Here you can immerse yourself in the vibrant traditions and rich narrative of the Cherokee people in so many ways.

The Oconaluftee Indian Village provides an engaging look into 18th-century Cherokee life. This living history museum features authentic Cherokee dwellings, artisans demonstrating ancient crafts, and sacred ritual sites guided tours that bring the past to life.

Dive deeper at the Museum of the Cherokee People, where more than 11,000 years of Cherokee history is told through interactive exhibits showcasing artifacts, art, and stories. Additionally, the Qualla Arts and Crafts Mutual, Inc., is the nation's oldest Native American cooperative. You'll find a variety of handcrafted items, from pottery to beadwork.

Make sure you secure tickets to see the *Unto These Hills* outdoor drama, a powerful theatrical production that tells the story of the Cherokee from their origins, through the Trail of Tears, and to the modern day where they continue to thrive and shape their own future. The production runs seasonally from late May to late August, with nightly performances, except Sundays.

TIP

While in Cherokee, check out the Judaculla Rock. The soapstone boulder features intricate petroglyph carvings believed to date back thousands of years and is named for the Cherokee legend of Judaculla, a giant with supernatural powers. The engravings are attributed to the Cherokee people and feature approximately 1,548 designs, including humanlike figures, animal shapes, and abstract patterns, thought to represent spiritual or ceremonial significance.

498 Tsali Blvd., Cherokee
visitcherokeenc.com

82

STEP INTO HISTORY AND MORE IN NEW BERN

Situated at the confluence of the Neuse and Trent Rivers, New Bern boasts a rich history as one of the state's oldest towns. Swiss and German immigrants settled the land in 1710, naming it after Bern, the capital of Switzerland. Long before the Europeans arrived, however, the Tuscarora Indians lived along New Bern's riverbanks in a village they called Chattoka.

This picturesque city served as North Carolina's colonial capital and played a pivotal role in the American Revolution and Civil War. Costumed guides lead visitors through the remarkable Tryon Palace, a reconstructed 18th-century governor's mansion surrounded by lush gardens, offering an immersive glimpse into colonial life.

Other historic stops include the New Bern Firemen's Museum, home to vintage fire engines and artifacts that showcase the city's firefighting legacy. Refresh yourself with a visit to the Birthplace of Pepsi, a soda shop and museum located on the spot where Caleb Bradham invented the iconic soft drink in 1898.

Wander along the tree-lined streets of historic downtown New Bern in search of treasures. Shops and galleries brim with antiques, art, locally made crafts, and other distinct items.

NEW BERN STOPS

Tryon Palace

529 S Front St., New Bern, 800-767-1560
tryonpalace.org

New Bern Firemen's Museum

420 Broad St., New Bern, 252-636-4087
newbernfiremuseum.com

The Birthplace of Pepsi

256 Middle St., New Bern, 252-636-5898

DID YOU KNOW?

Nicholas Sparks fans will likely recognize many local landmarks. New Bern is the author's adopted hometown and the setting for some of his most popular novels. *The Wedding*, *A Bend in the Road*, *The Return*, and *The Notebook* are all set in New Bern.

83

TOUR "AMERICA'S LARGEST HOME"
AT BILTMORE ESTATE

Located in Asheville and ringed by the Blue Ridge Mountains, Biltmore Estate was the ambitious vision of George Washington Vanderbilt III, grandson of railroad and steamship magnate Cornelius Vanderbilt.

After Vanderbilt visited the area in 1888, he was so smitten with the climate and vistas, he purchased 125,000 acres and began construction on his "little mountain escape" in 1889. The 250-room French Renaissance château stands as a testament to Gilded Age grandeur, with its opulent architecture, priceless art, and antiques across its 175,000 square feet.

Highlights of a tour include the 70-foot-high banquet hall with its massive triple fireplaces, a library holding 10,000 volumes, a basement featuring the original kitchen, and an indoor swimming pool.

The meticulously maintained gardens were designed by the famous landscape architect Frederick Law Olmsted, the same mind behind New York City's Central Park. Extend your Biltmore Estate experience with an overnight stay at the Village Hotel, The Inn on Biltmore Estate, or in the restored historic Cottages on Biltmore Estate.

1 Lodge St., Asheville, 800-411-3812
biltmore.com

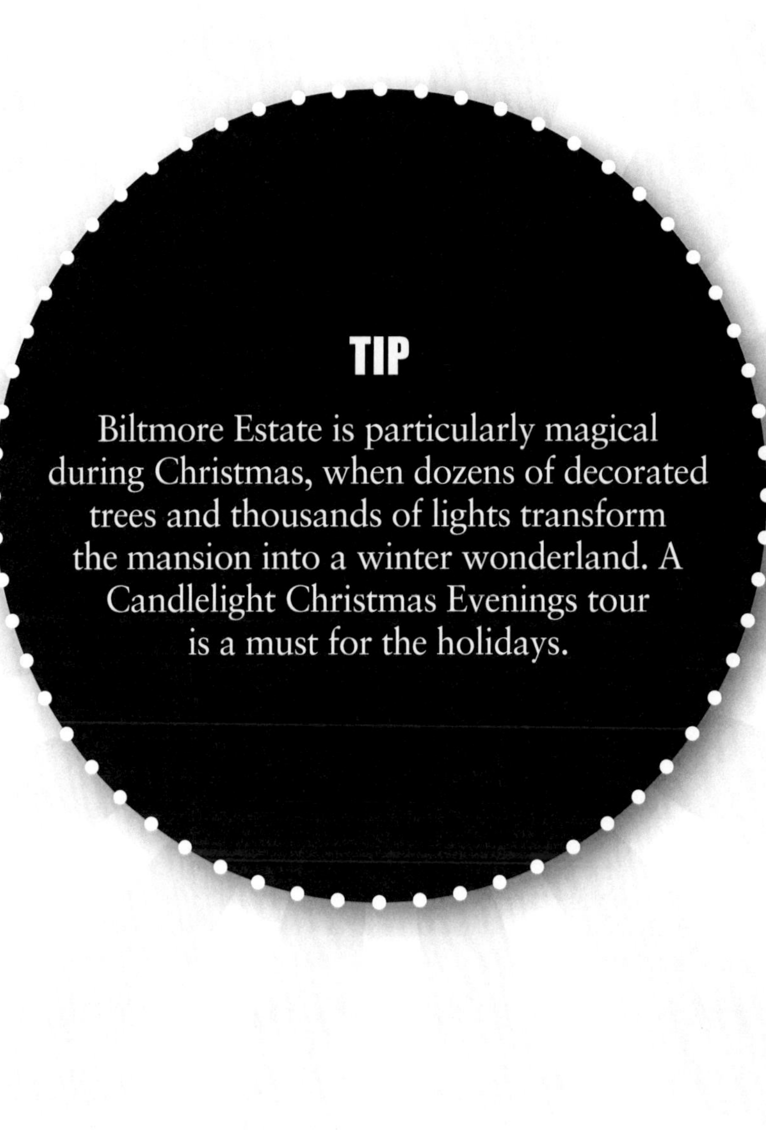

TIP

Biltmore Estate is particularly magical during Christmas, when dozens of decorated trees and thousands of lights transform the mansion into a winter wonderland. A Candlelight Christmas Evenings tour is a must for the holidays.

GET ARTSY
AROUND THE STATE

North Carolina is blessed with a solid selection of art museums, with many holding historical artifacts and paintings from around the globe.

In Charlotte, the Mint Museum showcases American, European, and contemporary art. Nearby, the Harvey B. Gantt Center for African-American Arts + Culture highlights African American art, history, and culture. The Bechtler Museum of Modern Art focuses on mid-20th-century modern art, featuring works by Picasso, Warhol, and others.

North Carolina Museum of Art in Raleigh is one of the Southeast's premier visual arts museums. With a permanent collection that spans more than 5,000 years, there's plenty to soak in—classical European works, African art, and outdoor installations in its 164-acre museum park.

Peruse American art from the colonial period to contemporary works, featuring paintings, sculptures, and decorative arts at Winston-Salem's Reynolda House Museum of American Art.

In Asheville, the Folk Art Center is headquarters for the Southern Highland Craft Guild, made up of more than 900 juried artists from across the Southeast, and the River Arts District is home to artist studios and galleries in a revitalized industrial area. Hurricane Helene caused significant flooding here in 2024, but the district has rebounded, showcasing resilience through its dynamic art scene.

EXPERIENCE NORTH CAROLINA ART

Mint Museum

500 S Tryon St., Charlotte
704-337-2000
mintmuseum.org

Harvey B. Gantt Center for African-American Arts + Culture

551 S Tryon St., Charlotte
704-547-3700
ganttcenter.org

Bechtler Museum of Modern Art

420 S Tryon St., Charlotte
704-353-9209
bechtler.org

North Carolina Museum of Art

2110 Blue Ridge Rd., Raleigh
919-839-6262
ncartmuseum.org

Reynolda House

2250 Reynolda Rd., Winston-Salem
336-758-5584
reynolda.org

Folk Art Center

Milepost 382, Blue Ridge Pkwy., Asheville
828-523-4110
southernhighlandguild.org

River Arts District

Asheville, riverartsdistrict.com

GET STARSTRUCK
AT THE AVA GARDNER MUSEUM

Before she became a film legend, Ava Gardner was a small-town North Carolina girl. She was born in the tiny farm community of Grabtown, just outside Smithfield in Johnston County.

Gardner appeared in several films before capturing critics' notice with her performance in the film noir *The Killers* in 1946. She went on to star in major films such as *Show Boat*, *The Snows of Kilimanjaro*, *The Sun Also Rises*, and *The Night of the Iguana*, earning Oscar, Golden Globe, and BAFTA nominations.

The Ava Gardner Museum in downtown Smithfield pays homage to the iconic actress and her work. It's home to a robust collection of artifacts from Gardner's private life and 45-year career. Exhibits showcase movie costumes, dresses, and gowns worn by Gardner, as well as original scripts, photos, posters, and personal items.

For a more in-depth Ava Gardner experience, time your visit with the Ava Gardner Festival. The annual festival takes place in early October and features movie screenings, presentations and discussions, and breakfast at the museum.

325 E Market St., Smithfield, 919-934-5830
johnstoncountync.org/ava-gardner

VISIT THE HOME
OF THE "POET OF THE PEOPLE"

The charming mountain village of Flat Rock has many allures—one of which is the Carl Sandburg Home National Historic Site, which preserves the home of the Pulitzer Prize–winning poet and author.

Sandburg previously lived in Illinois, Wisconsin, and Michigan. However, he settled his family in the quiet mountain town of Flat Rock in 1945, making his home on the 246-acre estate Connemara. It was a more desirable location for his wife and daughter to raise dairy goats. The home, originally constructed in 1838, anchors the Carl Sandburg Home National Historic Site. It's filled with the Sandburgs' furnishings as they lived at Connemara from 1945–1968, including Carl Sandburg's personal collection of 12,000 books.

You can wander along five miles of hiking trails on the Connemara property (from easy to moderate). The big treat for most visitors, though, are the goats. Mrs. Sandburg owned and operated a premier goat dairy and bred champion goats. Some on the property today descended from Mrs. Sandburg's famous herd.

The Carl Sandburg Home National Historic Site really is the sweet spot for those interested in both literary history and natural beauty.

81 Carl Sandburg Ln., Flat Rock, 828-693-4178
nps.gov/carl/index.htm

87

STEP INTO
THE ANDY GRIFFITH SHOW IN MOUNT AIRY

Mount Airy is a charming hamlet that offers visitors a taste of Americana with its rich history and friendly atmosphere. Fans of *The Andy Griffith Show* will feel right at home here. It's the birthplace of actor Andy Griffith and the inspiration for the classic television series. The town's streets and landmarks echo the fictional setting of Mayberry, from the courthouse square to the iconic Wally's Service Station. Guided tours are a great way to bring the memorable show to life, especially when you do so from the back of a vintage squad car that even Barney Fife would be proud to drive. Don't miss the Andy Griffith Museum, with memorabilia from the show, or the Mayberry Courthouse and Jail, which features Deputy Barney Fife's desk and Andy Taylor's office. Grab a sweet treat and a touch of nostalgia at Opie's Candy Store.

Mount Airy
visitmayberry.com

Squad Car Tours
625 S Main St., Mount Airy
336-789-OPIE (6743)
tourmayberry.com

TIP

Spring for a butler tour, which you can reserve online when you book your stay. The roughly hour-and-a-half tour offers fascinating details about the property's history.

YELL "ALL ABOARD!"
AT TWEETSIE RAILROAD

Tweetsie dates back to 1882, when the East Tennessee and Western North Carolina Railroad started up in Johnson City, Tennessee. It earned its name from locals who became accustomed to the shrill "tweet" of the train's whistles. Locomotive No. 12 was constructed in 1917 as one of the 13 narrow-gauge ET&WNC steam locomotives. When rail service to Boone ceased in 1940, all steam locomotives were sold or scrapped—except for No. 12. Meticulously restored and listed on the National Register of Historic Places, Tweetsie's No. 12 continues to delight rail fans of all ages. It opened as a theme park in 1957—North Carolina's first—and features Western-themed rides where costumed actors provide an exciting adventure along the way.

300 Tweetsie Railroad Ln.
Blowing Rock, 800-526-5740
tweetsie.com

215 Tweetsie Railroad Ln.
Blowing Rock, 828-266-0176
highgravityadventures.com

TIP

When your time at Tweetsie Railroad concludes, head next door to High Gravity Adventures, which offers multiple zip lines, a sky bridge, and 1,700 feet of zipping. I highly recommend adding the Giant Swing to your tour. The giant pendulum swing pulls you up 45 feet, then you pull the ripcord to release it. I can't remember when I've scream-laughed so hard!

89

WALK ON THE WILD SIDE
AT THE MUSEUM OF THE BIZARRE

If you have a penchant for all things weird and wonderful, add the Museum of the Bizarre to your Wilmington itinerary. Opened by Justin LaNasa in 2015, this eclectic museum teems with all sorts of unique artifacts, oddities, and unusual props.

There's plenty to see within the 2,500-square-foot building. Alexander Hamilton's hair, a possessed clown, the Fort Fisher mermaid, and Houdini's Ouija board, among other oddities, are on display. Kids will go bananas over the Laser Vault Maze. Green beams of light fill the room, and you must stealthily navigate your way around without touching them. During select times on weekends, you might even get to witness a sword swallowing demonstration. The museum also hosts science workshops, lectures, and various special exhibits throughout the year.

201 S Water St., Wilmington, 910-399-2641
museumbizarre.com

90

ENJOY A "PURRFECT" VISIT TO THE AMERICAN MUSEUM OF THE HOUSE CAT

Leonardo da Vinci once said, "The smallest feline is a masterpiece." I believe if a time machine were on the list of da Vinci's inventions, he would have used it to visit the American Museum of the House Cat in the 21st century.

Situated in the mountain town of Sylva, the museum is dedicated entirely to—you guessed it—cats. It was established in 2017 by Dr. Harold Sims, who sadly passed away in late 2024. Dr. Sims was affectionately known as "Cat Man," and the museum showcases his extensive 35-plus-year collection of cat-related art, memorabilia, curiosities, and antiques.

More than 5,000 items are on display here, including a medieval-era petrified cat and a 2,600-year-old bronze of the feline goddess Bastet. After your museum tour, hit the gift shop for T-shirts, cat toys, books, jewelry, and other souvenirs.

The museum operates from April through December, welcoming guests Mondays through Saturdays from 10 a.m. to 5 p.m., and Sundays from noon to 5 p.m. Proceeds fund the Catman2 Cat Shelter, a no-kill cat shelter founded by Dr. Sims.

5063 US Hwy. 441 S, Sylva, 828-476-9376
wnccatmuseum.org

91

TAKE A SPIN
AROUND THE VOLLIS SIMPSON WHIRLIGIG PARK

The Vollis Simpson Whirligig Park is a captivating outdoor museum that showcases the whimsical world of wind-driven art created by folk artist Vollis Simpson. It features more than 30 colorful, towering whirligigs, each a testament to Simpson's imagination and mechanical genius. Simpson, a self-taught artist and engineer, created these kinetic sculptures from salvaged materials, blending art and engineering into vibrant masterpieces.

The park's centerpiece attractions are the monumental whirligigs, some reaching over 50 feet tall. These intricate structures spin and twirl with the wind, creating a mesmerizing display of movement and color. The park also hosts a visitor center, providing insights into Simpson's life and creative process.

301 Goldsboro St. S, Wilson, 252-674-1352
wilsonwhirligigpark.org

TIP

The Whirligig Museum and Gift Shop is open Tuesdays through Saturdays from 10 a.m. to 5 p.m.

FIND INSPIRATION
IN THE KINDRED SPIRIT MAILBOX

On a secluded stretch of coastline within Bird Island Reserve on Sunset Beach, the Kindred Spirit Mailbox is a singular experience for those seeking solitude and reflection. It was erected in the mid-1970s by Frank Nesmith and Claudia Sailor, who aimed to create a space where visitors could leave notes, letters, and journals, expressing their thoughts, dreams, and reflections.

The original mailbox, simply marked "Kindred Spirit," quickly became a cherished tradition and even provided inspiration for Nicholas Sparks's 2018 novel *Every Breath*. The mailbox has been replaced several times over the years due to weathering, but the spirit of it remains unchanged. Visitors continue to flock to this secluded spot, walking along the pristine beach, to leave behind their writings or read the entries left by others.

The Kindred Spirit Mailbox represents a living anthology of personal stories, hopes, and shared human connection, offering a testament to the enduring power of community and introspection amid nature's tranquility.

facebook.com/BirdIslandKindredSpirit

TIP

Park at the 40th Street public beach access near the Sunset Beach Pier. From there, it's about a 1.5-mile walk southwest to reach the mailbox.

WINSTON SALEM
THE JOY OF CONSENT
MANON GARCIA
LOVE
A GOOD READ
INDIES
RIDERS QUADRANT
BOOKISH CATS
REBECCA YARROS
ONYX STORM
FOURTH WING
Basgiath
War College

Bookmarks

SHOPPING AND FASHION

PERUSE LOCALLY MADE POTTERY IN SEAGROVE

The town of Seagrove earned the moniker "The Handmade Pottery Capital of the United States" for good reason. It spans almost 30 miles along Highway 705 and is the country's largest concentration of working potters. The region has drawn potters since the 18th century thanks to the area's quality of clay and the abundance of trees to supply firewood for heating kilns.

Here you can marvel at the wide range of distinctive and gorgeous pottery at more than 50 working studios: contemporary, folk art, historical pieces, and functional dinnerware. Throughout the year, studios host various events and open houses, providing the chance to witness these gifted artisans at work. The area's signature event is November's weekend-long Celebration of Seagrove Potters.

Don't miss a single studio! Go to the Seagrove Pottery website and download a PDF map or use an interactive version with all the studio locations.

TIP

Make the North Carolina Pottery Center the first stop on your Seagrove Pottery tour. It's an ideal primer, providing a wealth of information about the roots of pottery in North Carolina.

DISCOVER TREASURES
AT THE RALEIGH MARKET

The North Carolina State Fair isn't the only time to visit the fairgrounds in Raleigh. Every Saturday and Sunday since 1971, it's a shopping mecca. Rain or shine, hundreds of vendors are on hand, offering a cornucopia of goods. You'll find everything from antiques, art, and furniture to clothing, collectibles, and jewelry. Admission and parking are free, so you'll have even more money to buy that necklace that speaks to you or the set of golf clubs you've been searching for. And if you work up an appetite from deal hunting, various food trucks and farm stands are on-site to keep you sated.

4285 Trinity Rd., Raleigh, 919-839-4560
theraleighmarket.com

95

STEP BACK IN TIME
AT MAST GENERAL STORE

Acclaimed travel journalist Charles Kuralt once said, "Where should I send you to know the soul of the South? I think I'll send you to the Mast General Store."

The original Mast General Store is situated in the modest, scenic mountain community of Valle Crucis—the state's first rural historic district. Dating back to 1883, the store teems with nostalgia. As you walk along the creaking floorboards perusing shelves, you'll find a bounty of mountain town essentials, old-fashioned candy, speckleware, country gourmet foods, cast iron cookware, and much more.

Asheville's Mast General Store also has historic roots. It's in an 1846 building that housed many businesses throughout the years. You can spy remnants of the structure's life as Fain's Thrift Store (1946) as soon as you enter. The original terrazzo inlaid tile from Fain's is at the front of the store.

Additional Mast General outposts are in Waynesville, Hendersonville, and Winston-Salem. If you travel outside the Tar Heel State, look for one in Greenville and Columbia, South Carolina, and in Knoxville, Tennessee.

mastgeneralstore.com

MAST GENERAL STORE LOCATIONS

15 Biltmore Ave., Asheville, 828-232-1883

63 N Main St., Waynesville, 828-452-2101

516 Trade St. NW, Hendersonville, 828-696-1883

516 N Trade St., Winston-Salem, 336-727-2015

96

SNAG A BARGAIN AT THRIFT STORES

Scouring local thrift stores is top of my list of activities no matter where I travel within the Tar Heel State. I'm always on the hunt for a great deal on embroidered handkerchiefs or a brightly colored caftan that gives me all the Mrs. Roper vibes.

From vintage Halloween decorations and brass candleholders to pristine Dean Martin albums and adorable bedazzled purses, you never know what treasure you'll find. North Carolina teems with great thrifting spots in mountain hamlets, cities, and oceanfront towns. Whether you're looking for that perfect jean jacket or wanting to add unique art to your living room gallery wall, there are so many fun consignment stores to check out!

TIP

Did you discover your best thrift find yet? Share your North Carolina thrifting wins with me on Instagram! Use #100ThingsNC.

GET THRIFTY

Sleepy Poet Antique Mall

6424 South Blvd., Charlotte, 704-529-6369
sleepypoetstuff.com

Reconsidered Goods

4118 Spring Garden St., Greensboro, 336-763-5041
reconsideredgoods.org

North Raleigh Ministries

9650 Strickland Rd., Raleigh
2821 Brentwood Rd., Raleigh
919-844-6676
northraleighministries.com/thrift-shoppes

The Rose Thrift and More

108 S Center St., Hickory, 828-855-2944
facebook.com/Therosethriftandmore

P.A.W.S. Resale Shoppe

5941 Carolina Beach Rd., Wilmington, 910-399-8390
facebook.com/pawsresaleshoppe

Animal Haven of Asheville

65 Lower Grassy Branch Rd., 828-299-1635
animalhavenofasheville.org

97

EMBARK

ON A NORTH CAROLINA INDIE BOOKSTORE CRAWL

When it comes to reading, I'm proudly old school. One of the best ways to spend an afternoon is with my nose in a book, thumbing through its pages and highlighting memorable sections and quotes. Wherever I travel, I'll likely make my way to a local bookstore (or 10) and peruse the shelves for my next favorite read.

From seaside shops to mountain book nooks, North Carolina feeds my inner book nerd remarkably well. And a local bookstore crawl is a fantastic way to explore new cities and towns, as well as to support local economies.

UNC Greensboro University Libraries, in partnership with the Institute of Museum Library and Services and the State Library of North Carolina, created a comprehensive list of independent bookstores throughout the state. You can find the Independent Bookstores list at libapps4.uncg.edu/nclitmap/bookstores.

TIP

Schedule your indie bookstore tour around Independent Bookstore Day. This national event typically takes place on the last Saturday in April. However, local bookstores celebrate all month, often featuring special promotions and sweet deals on books.

BOOKSTORES TO EXPLORE

Park Road Books

4139 Park Rd., Charlotte, 704-525-9239
parkroadbooks.com

Battery Park Book Exchange & Champagne Bar

1 Page Ave., #101, Asheville, 828-252-0020
batteryparkbookexchange.com

Bookmarks

634 W 4th St., #110, Winston-Salem, 336-747-1471
bookmarksnc.org

Scuppernong Books

304 S Elm St., Greensboro, 336-763-1919
scuppernongbooks.com

McIntyre's Books in Fearrington

220 Market St., Pittsboro, 919-542-3030
fearrington.com/mcintyres-books

Quail Ridge Books

4209-100 Lassiter Mill Rd., Raleigh, 919-828-1588
quailridgebooks.com

Books to Be Red

34 School Rd., Ocracoke, 252-928-3936
ocracokebookstore.com

Plott Hound Books

102 W Main St., Burnsville, 828-536-5175
plotthoundbooks.com

Highland Books

36 W Main St., Brevard, 828-884-2424
highlandbooksonline.com

HUNT FOR FURNITURE AND MORE

IN HIGH POINT

If you're on the hunt for a new dining room set or a coffee table, High Point is the place to go.

Known globally as the "Furniture Capital of the World," High Point has been the epicenter of American furniture manufacturing and design since the late 19th century. The High Point Market, held twice yearly, is the largest home furnishings industry trade show in the world, transforming the city into a bustling hub of design professionals and furniture buyers from over 100 countries.

High Point offers plenty of amusements beyond furniture hunting. For example, the High Point Museum offers fascinating exhibits about the region's furniture-making history and Piedmont culture. Additionally, the Nido & Mariana Qubein Children's Museum is ideal for a family outing. It's home to immersive hands-on exhibits, an outdoor Adventure Zone, plus the Hall of Mysteries, where you can explore secret passages, find clues, and solve a variety of mysteries

High Point Museum
1859 E Lexington Ave., High Point, 336-885-1859
highpointnc.gov/3078/museum

Nido & Mariana Qubein Children's Museum
200 Qubein Ave., High Point, 336-888-7529
qubeinchildrensmuseum.org

SAY "OUI, S'IL VOUS PLAÎT!" TO SHOPPING AT DE PROVENCE ET D'AILLEURS

Step into this charming shop in Blowing Rock, and you might feel like you've been transported to the lavender fields and sun-drenched landscapes of Provence. Roughly translated, De Provence et D'Ailleurs means "from Provence and elsewhere." Owner and operator Danielle de Ville d'Avray Tester is originally from the Provence region of France. She's been providing an authentic touch of France to the mountains for nearly 30 years.

This charming shop is a Francophile's mecca, offering imported French household goods, gourmet foods, and artisanal crafts all carefully curated to bring the essence of Provence to the North Carolina mountains.

It is a sensory delight. Hand-painted Provençal tablecloths in vibrant blues and yellows hang alongside woven market baskets. Glass jars filled with fragrant herbs and lavender line rustic tables, while handcrafted soaps, olive oils, and local honey fill antique cabinets.

131-8 Morris St., Blowing Rock, 828-295-9989
facebook.com/pages/De-Provence-Et-Dailleurs/157989417565777

100

APPRECIATE LOCAL ARTISTS
AT PIEDMONT CRAFTSMEN

In the heart of Winston-Salem's thriving Arts District, Piedmont Craftsmen, Inc. transformed the city's cultural landscape by establishing a guild dedicated to fine craft excellence. Founded in 1963, this non-profit organization showcases and promotes the work of juried craftspeople, ensuring exceptional quality and originality.

The organization's headquarters serves as both gallery and community centerpiece. It houses an exceptional collection of contemporary and traditional crafts from over 350 juried member artists. You'll find handcrafted jewelry, ceramics, textiles, wood furnishings, glass art, and metal works.

Their signature event, the Piedmont Craftsmen's Fair held each November, attracts thousands of collectors and art enthusiasts to meet artists and purchase one-of-a-kind works.

Beyond sales, Piedmont Craftsmen nurtures emerging talent through education programs and exhibitions, maintaining its position as a vital cultural institution that bridges traditional techniques with contemporary artistic vision in the Southeast.

601 North Trade St., Winston-Salem, 336-725-1516
piedmontcraftsmen.org

ACTIVITIES
BY SEASON

WINTER

SPRING

SUMMER

FALL

Old Salem

Seagrove Pottery
Credit HeartofNorthCarolina.com

SUGGESTED ITINERARIES

FAMILY FUN

FOODIES

FANS OF THE ARTS

OUTDOORSY TYPES

HISTORY BUFFS

Crabtree Falls

Oak Island Lighthouse
Credit North Carolina's Brunswick Islands

INDEX